# PRAISE FOR *ATTACKING ANXIETY*

"This is not a book, it is a call to arms. If you feel like you are losing the battle that is anxiety, it is now time to fight back. My friend Shawn Johnson will show you how. This is not a collection of theories, it is a war-torn, battle-proven playbook that he has employed in the midst of his personal hand-to-hand combat with panic that will give you tools you need to thrive in your own fight. I have called Shawn on the darkest of days and his encouragement to me is what he will share with you if you let him."

—LEVI LUSKO, LEAD PASTOR OF FRESH LIFE
CHURCH AND BESTSELLING AUTHOR

"When you find yourself at the end of yourself, Shawn doesn't just give you inspiration—he gives you *application*. As a leader navigating uncertainty in work and life, Shawn's wisdom and practical insights have been a gift in this season! His simple yet profound words are a playbook on how to handle anxiety and attack it with supernatural strength."

—BIANCA JUAREZ OLTHOFF, PASTOR, BESTSELLING
AUTHOR, AND PODCAST HOST OF *WE'RE GOING THERE*

"I've been privileged to walk with Shawn Johnson during some of his battles with anxiety, and his courage, faith, and reliance on God's power continue to inspire me. *Attacking Anxiety* is so much more than Shawn's story—it's a hands-on, in-the-trenches survival manual for anyone experiencing this crippling condition that affects millions of people around the world. Shawn discovered resources that help him fight back and now shares a battle plan to help all of us enjoy the freedom we have in Christ. A must-read!"

—CHRIS HODGES, SENIOR PASTOR OF CHURCH OF THE HIGHLANDS
AND AUTHOR OF *THE DANIEL DILEMMA* AND *OUT OF THE CAVE*

"The feeling of intense fear when anxiety and depression close in on our minds and hearts is unbearable, and often times traps our minds into believing that God is not in this fight with us. Shawn's story is one of God's grace in the midst of unbelievable anxiety and depression, and it's also one of winning, if you choose to not give up. This book is a refreshing and encouraging guide to fighting back, to not letting anxiety and depression define us, and to trusting God with complete joy."

—CHAD VEACH, FOUNDER AND LEAD PASTOR OF ZOE CHURCH, AUTHOR, AND HOST OF THE *LEADERSHIP LEAN IN* PODCAST

"In our current culture where depression and anxiety are at an all-time high, *Attacking Anxiety* comes at just the right time. This book is the perfect resource to read if you, like me, have battled anxiousness, loss of control, or even the inability to cope. Pastor Shawn dives into how we can live a life where anxiety isn't our label or our future. He shows us that we don't have to just sit back and let it attack us, we can choose to fight back—with the weapons of God's Word—and overcome the anxiety monster once and for all and live the life God always intended for us to live: free."

—MADISON PREWITT, TELEVISION PERSONALITY

"Anxiety is running amuck everywhere we turn. We're anxious about the future, the past, about our family, our lives, and it seems to be inescapable. It's as if we are in a pit looking up, ill-prepared and unprotected from an oppressive enemy. There is hope, but you cannot do it alone! In this book, Shawn has a thoughtful and inspired approach to help you face your fears and find calm in the chaos, step-by-step. Get ready to discover how to stand up, fight back, and unleash the peace of God in your life!"

—ED YOUNG, FOUNDER AND SENIOR PASTOR OF FELLOWSHIP CHURCH, AUTHOR, AND CONFERENCE SPEAKER

"Whenever Pastor Shawn speaks, you should listen. He uses real-life situations that we all can understand, while also referencing Scripture to paint a clear picture of the message coming from it. He has the ability to make everyone feel welcomed and accepted while withholding judgement—'we are all imperfect people pursuing a perfect God.'"

—SHAQUIL BARRETT, TWO-TIME SUPER BOWL CHAMPION

"My brother Shawn has helped change my life in more ways than he even knows. His realness and authenticity are inspiring to everyone who knows him, and his story is relatable to us all!"

—MICHAEL PORTER JR., PROFESSIONAL BASKETBALL PLAYER

# ATTACKING
# *ANXIETY*

## From Panicked and Depressed
## to *ALIVE* and *FREE*

## SHAWN JOHNSON

NELSON
BOOKS

An Imprint of Thomas Nelson

### Library of Congress Cataloging-in-Publication Data

Names: Johnson, Shawn, author.
Title: Attacking anxiety: from panicked and depressed to alive and free / Shawn Johnson.
Description: Nashville, Tennessee: Nelson Books, [2022] | Summary: "Shawn Johnson, lead pastor of Red Rocks Church, gives a searingly honest portrait of anxiety and depression and shows readers how to fight back and live free"-- Provided by publisher.
Identifiers: LCCN 2021032006 (print) | LCCN 2021032007 (ebook) | ISBN 9781400230693 | ISBN 9781400230709 (epub)
Subjects: LCSH: Anxiety--Religious aspects--Christianity. | Depression, Mental--Religious aspects--Christianity. | Depressed persons--Religious life.
Classification: LCC BV4908.5 .J645 2022 (print) | LCC BV4908.5 (ebook) | DDC 152.4/6--dc23
LC record available at https://lccn.loc.gov/2021032006
LC ebook record available at https://lccn.loc.gov/2021032007

*Printed in the United States of America*

22 23 24 25 26  BRR  10 9 8 7 6 5 4 3 2 1

*To my wife, Jill, and our three boys, Ethan, Austin, and Ashton: without the four of you in my life, I'm not sure I would be here today. I can't thank you enough for your love, support, and encouragement. I love you so much it hurts.*

*To anyone who finds themselves dealing with anxiety, depression, or hopelessness: if it seems like the darkness may never go away, I know how you feel. But I'm living proof that God can change lives. And my prayer for you is that my story will help you find more peace, joy, confidence, and freedom than you ever thought possible.*

# CONTENTS

# CONTENTS

## PART 3: STOP

## PART 4: REMEMBER

# FOREWORD

## by Craig Groeschel

Pastor Shawn Johnson is different.

Very different.

When I say Shawn is different, I don't mean in a this-person-is-really-strange-so-I-better-be-careful-around-him type of way. I'm talking about a very rare and special kind of different. The moment I met Shawn, I knew he was the real deal. It was impossible to miss.

I love that Shawn is raw. He is *always* raw. (If you don't believe me, keep reading. You'll see I'm not exaggerating.) He's also gut-wrenchingly honest, even if it would be better for him to tone down what's true.

Shawn is humble. Almost too humble. (Can a person be too humble?) He is down-to-earth, relatable, and has incredible compassion for the most broken. Shawn's got a genuine love for God that is neither annoying nor overly religious. His relationship with God is sincere. His love for God is contagious.

Even though Shawn is an amazing husband, world-class dad, and the founding pastor of one of America's greatest churches, he is not a superhero. He's very human. In fact, for years this very special, unusually humble, sincerely godly man struggled with a hidden burden.

Shawn battled ongoing, crippling, life-altering anxiety.

At one point, when most thought Shawn was on top of the world, his inner life was falling apart. The pressure and anxiety became more than his body could bear, and Shawn hit bottom. Hard.

I remember talking to him and his wife, Jill, like it was yesterday. Every word he uttered felt filled with fear. Through tears he cried out, terrified he'd hit a point of no return.

My wife and I were honored to be close to Shawn's family and to watch the work of God unfold. Over the next months, Shawn submitted himself to ongoing professional help. With the assistance of trained counselors and experts, he traveled a raw and rocky journey of exploration into abuse from his past and new ways to experience the grace of God in the present.

I won't make the process sound easier than it was. The journey was hell. (I think that's exactly how Shawn described it to me midway through his treatment.) But as Shawn faced the pain, the pressure, and his past, a theme started to emerge. Because it was what he'd always known, Shawn had assumed overwhelming anxiety was his lot in life. It was the cross he had to bear. But Shawn slowly realized the time had come to stop thinking of himself as a victim. God was calling him to stand up and fight back. And fight back he did.

With new spiritual tools and an army of loving support, Shawn started to take back the ground he hadn't known he could gain. Day after day, he fought for peace, joy, and freedom.

The Shawn I know today is different.

He's still different in the good-kind-of-different way I described earlier.

But now he's also different in a different kind of way.

He's at peace.

He's full of joy.

With God's help, he's in the fight for full freedom from anxiety.

As a fellow pastor, I know so many people hurt like Shawn. Too many silently suffer with uncontrollable bouts of anxiety, panic, and angst. Like Shawn, they feel sentenced to—and imprisoned in—a life of hopelessness. That's why I encouraged Shawn to write this book. God's work in him and his family is too important not to share.

If you battle anxiety, let me offer you both a warning and some encouragement. First, a word of caution. Get ready for some real talk. Remember, Shawn is raw. You'll likely hurt with him. You may be tempted to stop reading when his story gets too close to your own. Please don't. Because Shawn is also honest, humble, and godly. And what he's learned about attacking anxiety is powerful. It's inspiring enough to motivate you, practical enough to equip you, and loving enough to reassure you.

As you know, the darkness feels darker than most would ever understand. But Shawn will help you see how the light of Jesus can shine into your darkness and transform you from panicked and depressed to alive and free.

Craig Groeschel
founder and lead pastor of Life.Church,
author of *Winning the War in Your Mind*

# INTRODUCTION

## *I Need a Miracle*

"Honey, what's wrong?"

My wife's voice rang through the speakers in my truck as she tried to calm me down. I could barely see the cars in front of me through the tears in my eyes.

"Shawn, where are you? Can you make it home?"

I didn't know what to say.

I didn't know what to do.

I didn't know what was happening or why it was happening to me.

All I knew was that I needed a miracle.

"I'm on C-470," I said between sharp breaths. "But I don't think I can make it home. Please pray." Then I hung up the phone.

In retrospect, that was not the best way to end a call. But after twenty years of marriage, Jill knew exactly what was going on. I was having a panic attack and was quickly losing control. Although this wasn't my first panic attack, somehow Jill and I both knew this one was different.

This was the big one.

The first thing that happens when I'm having a panic attack is I start to feel extremely claustrophobic. The walls begin to cave in all around me, my chest tightens, and I feel like I'm suffocating. Next, my mind goes blurry, and I stop thinking straight. Then my skin feels like it's crawling, and all I know is I need to escape whatever environment I'm in.

It's one of the worst things I've ever felt in my life.

After that, the lies begin. A voice starts whispering in my ear, telling me this is it for me, that this current state is never going to end and that I'll spend the rest of my life in excruciating pain. If you've ever been there, you know that thought alone is enough to make you want to stop living.

On this particular day, the voice was reminding me I had nowhere to go. What would my staff think if I went to my office and they heard me cry? Leaders are supposed to have it all together. What would my neighbors think if I went home and they heard me scream? Most of them go to my church. Anywhere I went, people would be listening. People are always listening.

My mind was unable to formulate a plan. Between the panic attack and the claustrophobia, I was in no state to drive; I needed to get out of my truck. I pulled over to the side of the highway and started pacing back and forth at the base of the Rocky Mountains, right outside of Denver, Colorado.

From there, things got blurry. While cars drove by, I remember sobbing, then shouting, then screaming. Honestly, I don't even know who I was yelling at, probably God.

"Why won't you help me?"

"Why don't you care?"

"Why won't you fix me?"

"I can't live this way!"

"Where are you?"

"I need a miracle!"

Here's what you need to know about my life at that point. On paper, everything was amazing. I had the most incredible wife and three fantastic children, and I was the pastor of a large church. Everything about my life was going well, yet at that moment, I was ready to end it.

I found a small hill and sat down by the side of the highway, but I couldn't stop shaking and lost all sense of time. Nothing made sense. It felt like nobody would ever understand what I was going through. How could I be surrounded by such a terrific family and fantastic friends yet feel completely isolated?

*I must be crazy.*

*I'm losing my mind.*

*This is never going to end.*

*I'm going to be like this forever.*

*No one is ever going to truly understand.*

*Maybe I should kill myself.*

Eventually, my wife showed up with two of my friends, who were also coworkers. "I quit!" I shouted, before they could say a word. "I can't do this job anymore. I can't be a pastor. I can't handle the pressure. I don't want to keep living. I don't know what to do." They were trying to calm me down, but I couldn't hear it. I was humiliated and embarrassed.

"I'm sorry" was all I could think to say. And I meant it. "I'm sorry you're seeing me like this. I'm sorry I'm not better. I'm sorry I'm not stronger. I'm so sorry."

For some of you, what you just read felt extremely foreign. But for others, it hit way too close to home. Maybe you've experienced something similar, or perhaps you've watched a loved one suffer through something like this. Wherever you find yourself today, here's what I know: *mental health is a real issue, and it's time to start talking about it.*

By the time my friends got me home, I was exhausted. They sat me down at my kitchen table, but I couldn't stop shaking or crying. They kept telling me it was going to be okay. I kept trying to catch my breath. My chest was so tight that I felt like I was going to suffocate.

"You aren't thinking of doing anything stupid, are you?" they asked.

I knew the real question they were asking. They wanted to know if I was considering suicide.

"No," I said. "I'm not thinking that way."

Then I paused. My face fell. I couldn't believe it had gotten to this point. Trembling, I gave them the combo to the safe in my basement and asked them to take my guns—I wasn't sure I could trust myself. So, as my friends removed my weapons from my house, I sat there at my table, head in my hands, humiliated and so sick of feeling this way, whispering to God, "I need a miracle."

———

Have you ever had such bad anxiety or depression that you wondered if you could keep going? Have you ever experienced the humiliation of people you care about seeing you at your lowest point? Have you ever felt like you would do anything in the world to change how you are or the way you feel? Have you ever wanted to just disappear or felt like the people you care about would be better without you?

If you or someone you care about has ever felt anything like this, you are the reason I am writing this book. That's where I was. This book is about my journey from that place to where I am today.

I'm not writing from a place of perfection. I'm not writing to you from an ivory tower, saying I am completely 100 percent free from all anxiety and worry. And I'm certainly not writing to tell you I know the simple fix, the key to unlocking complete peace and joy with a few simple steps. In fact, I would question anyone who promises you that. We are all broken people, living in a broken world, and we won't experience absolute perfection until we get to heaven.

There are days when I can feel anxiety and depression trying to creep their way back into my life, and on those days, I still have to battle for my own freedom. The good news is that now I know how to do that. But like every single one of us, I'm still on a journey, and some days are better than others. But I can promise you this: I may not be where I *want* to be, but I am certainly not where I *used* to be.

I am writing to you today as someone who is healthier, stronger, and better than I was that day on the side of the road. I may know the depths of despair, but I also know the joy of true transformation. I have experienced the miraculous power of God working in my life in ways that I can't even comprehend. Today, I am experiencing peace, joy, confidence, and freedom at levels I thought were impossible for me. And I believe the same is possible for you right now.

I want you to know, right up top, that I believe you can experience freedom from anxiety and depression. You may have given up hope, but I believe you or your loved one can find levels of peace, joy, confidence, and freedom that will blow you away. Anxiety and depression can take us to a place of absolute hopelessness, convincing us that this pain will never end, never get better, and no one will ever understand. They try to convince us that this is our new reality and we just have to learn to deal with it. But I'm here to tell you that is a lie. You are not stuck like this. Trust me, this is *not* how your story ends!

Ephesians 3:20 tells us that God "is able to do immeasurably more than all we ask or imagine, according to his power that is at work within us." We have a God who does things that we never even thought possible. I am believing Ephesians 3:20 for you and your loved ones as you read this book.

In fact, if I could be so bold, I would like to challenge you to begin expecting God to show up for you in this way. Expect that God actually meant it when he said he was ready to do things in your life that you never dreamed possible. God wants to bring healing and restoration to your body, mind, and soul today.

The truth is, anxiety and depression are going to attack, but we can attack back! In this book, I'm going to talk to you about everything I've learned in my own battle with anxiety, depression, hopelessness, and even suicidal thoughts. If that sounds exhausting, remember the solution is not to pull yourself up by your bootstraps and force your way through this with your own strength. According to Ephesians 3:20, it is *his* power at work within us. If you (or a loved one) are at the end of your rope today, take heart; this book is about learning to let the God of the universe do the heavy lifting as he transforms your life.

Through this journey, God has done things that I could never do in my own strength. I am beginning to experience a level of freedom I never thought possible, and I'm telling you, this freedom is available to you as well. I want to show you what I've learned about standing firm and allowing the power of Christ to work in and through you. God created you to *live free*, and he is ready to heal you in ways you never thought possible.

If you are ready to dive in and find some freedom, pray this prayer with me:

*God, I pray right now for everyone who needs this book. I pray for them, their families, and everyone in this battle with them. Bring them hope. Give them the faith to believe that you can get involved, that you can intervene, that you can change things that we previously thought could never be changed and heal things that we thought could never be healed. God, I pray that you would help us live the life you called us to; help us step into a life of peace, joy, and purpose. I pray those reading would begin expecting you to set them free in ways they never thought possible. That they would be able to walk free, talk free, and truly live free. We thank you for this ahead of time in Jesus' name, amen.*

# 1

# LIVE FREE

Several years ago, my brother Paul spent two years in prison. When he got out, my family did what we do best—we threw him a party. We are from Kansas, and if there is one thing we know how to do, it's have a good time. I live out of state, so I missed out, but I certainly heard about it.

Aunt Jane, who threw the party, lived out in the country. She had one of those long dirt driveways leading up to her house, lined with barbwire fences on both sides to hold back the horses. At the end of the driveway, there was a big patch of dirt between her house and her barn, and that was the perfect place to celebrate.

Relatives came out of the woodwork.

If you had driven by Aunt Jane's house that day, you would've seen lawn chairs, coolers filled with Budweisers, homemade jean shorts with Skoal circles burned into the back pockets, NASCAR shirts (if the men were wearing shirts at all), and mullets—a whole lot of mullets.

You would have also noticed a very intense game of horse-shoes with a whole lot of yelling.

Yelling at one another.

Yelling at the kids as they ran by.

Yelling when someone hit a ringer.

And then in between all the shouting, you'd have heard laughter, some outrageous stories, and let's just call it *colorful* conversation.

In other words, if you'd driven by Aunt Jane's house that afternoon, you would have seen a full-on Kansas party.

But you would not have seen my brother Paul.

The entire thing was for him, but he wasn't participating. While the family was out front partying all day, Paul sat on the back porch by himself smoking cigarettes.

Everyone was celebrating his freedom—except him.

Sometime later, I asked him about that day, and he said one of the most profound things I've ever heard: "I was scared. I had been locked up for two years. I had to watch everything I did and every word I said. It was all I knew. I didn't know how to stand and talk to people; I didn't know what to say or how to act. It just terrified me, so I sat out back by myself."

Without knowing it, my brother was putting words to my experience and the experience of so many Christians I meet with. By law, my brother was a free man. The papers were signed; the deal was done.

Court adjourned.

He was free. But internally, he still felt like a prisoner. Paul was so used to being locked up that he didn't know how to function as a free man.

My brother had been *set free*, but he still didn't know how to *live free*.

And that sentence perfectly sums up how I felt as I sat crying on the side of the road that day. I knew the truth. I knew what Jesus did for me on the cross, dying to pay the price for my sins, setting me free for all of eternity. But there's a world of difference between being set free and being able to live free.

Have you ever found yourself sitting in the tension between those two places?

I can't tell you how many people I know who feel like they shouldn't struggle or be messed up because they are Christians or have a relationship of some kind with God. This misunderstanding is one of the primary sources of guilt and shame in a lot of people's lives.

*If I know God, how can I still deal with something like this? Aren't I supposed to be better? After all, Jesus set me free. How can I go to church, have a relationship with God, and still be this screwed up? I better not tell anybody. They'll never understand.*

It's that very mindset that begins to turn our anxiety and depression into internal prisons—prisons that no one can see but us.

This book is about learning to bridge the gap between being *set free* and actually being able to *live free*. Because if I've learned anything from the conversations, emails, DMs, and handwritten notes I receive every week—I'm not alone.

Statistically speaking, there's a good chance you or someone you know deals with anxiety or depression. And most counselors will tell you it's common that if you have one, you have the other.

Anxiety and depression go hand in hand.

You might struggle 99 percent of the time with one and 1 percent with the other, but they are both there. And let's be honest, some days it feels like you're struggling 100 percent with both. The Bible puts it like this: *"Anxiety* in the heart of man causes *depression"* (Proverbs 12:25 NKJV, emphasis added).

Whether you feel like you are dealing primarily with one or are drowning in both, let's just agree that we are in this together and that it is time for all of us to head in one direction: toward new levels of *freedom*!

# FOR FREEDOM

I get to stand up in front of Red Rocks Church on the weekends and tell people the best news in the world: Jesus died on the cross to set you free from sin and eternal separation from God. When we repent of our sins, choose to make him the Lord of our lives, and begin to follow him, we are *set free*.

And that's not just my opinion; God's Word promises that we are saved, forgiven, made perfect in God's sight, on our way to heaven forever, and eternally set free!

Every week we see person after person begin to understand that truth. And that's why we do what we do. In fact, our church's mission statement reads: "Red Rocks Church exists to make Heaven more crowded."[1]

But we can't stop there. If we do, we'll end up with a bunch of Christians who have been set free but have no idea how to live as if that is true.

When it comes to your anxiety, depression, and pending freedom, I want you to fully understand what God has promised you.

The apostle Paul wrote in his letter to his friends in Galatia, "It is for freedom that Christ has set us free. Stand firm, then, and do not let yourselves be burdened again by a yoke of slavery" (Galatians 5:1).

Did you catch that?

Galatians 5:1 is short, but it packs a punch. Paul could've started the fifth chapter of his letter by simply saying, "Christ has set us free." But he decided to take it a step further and remind his readers of the reason we all were set free.

*For freedom.*

We've been set free so that we can live free.

We've been set free eternally so that we can live free in the here and now.

The problem is, the *living free* part is not happening for many of us, is it?

Why is it so difficult to learn how to live free after being set free?

Why are the stats for mental illness in the church just as bad as they are for the rest of the world?

How come a pastor who makes a living telling people about being set free can end up pulled over on the side of the road, overwhelmed and ready to end it all?

Maybe you've been walking with Jesus for years but still find yourself riddled with anxiety. Maybe you've been blessed by God in so many ways but are still crippled by depression. Maybe your life looks perfect on paper, but you still find yourself held down by hopelessness. And let's be real: sometimes the fact that we have Jesus in our lives and still feel messed up makes it worse because we are ashamed to not be further along on our mental health journeys than we actually are.

Unfortunately, that's how *so many* of us are living our lives today. We've felt the isolation of anxiety and the confinement of depression for so long that these things are all we know. So, true freedom feels like a pipe dream.

We've been set free eternally by what Jesus did for us, but we're unable to live free and walk in the peace, joy, and confidence we've been given.

Listen to me—that is not God's plan for your life.

I promise.

In fact, that's not God's plan for anyone. God is very clear throughout Scripture that he wants us to experience freedom—and that it is actually attainable. Remember, I want you to know exactly what God promised you so that you can start to build up your faith. Freedom for you or your loved one is actually attainable!

### God Wants You to Experience: Peace

"Do not be anxious about anything, but in every situation, by prayer and petition, with thanksgiving, present your requests to God. And the peace of God, which transcends all understanding, will guard your hearts and your minds in Christ Jesus" (Philippians 4:6–7).

### God Wants You to Experience: Joy

"You make known to me the path of life; you will fill me with joy in your presence, with eternal pleasures at your right hand" (Psalm 16:11).

### God Wants You to Experience: Purpose

"He has saved us and called us to a holy life—not because of anything we have done but because of his own purpose and grace.

This grace was given us in Christ Jesus before the beginning of time" (2 Timothy 1:9).

### God Wants You to Experience: Confidence

"But blessed is the one who trusts in the Lord, whose confidence is in him" (Jeremiah 17:7).

### God Wants You to Experience: Protection

"But the Lord is faithful, and he will strengthen you and protect you from the evil one" (2 Thessalonians 3:3).

### God Wants You to Experience: Victory

"But thanks be to God! He gives us the victory through our Lord Jesus Christ" (1 Corinthians 15:57).

# STAND FIRM

What did you notice about those verses?

Hopefully, you saw that they represent the exact opposite of anxiety, depression, and hopelessness. Mental illness is not God's plan for your life. He wants you to *live free*.

Jesus died for you—not just to let you out of prison but so you could join the party!

In this book, we are about to get super practical and move forward together. And if you are feeling overwhelmed, don't worry—God will do the heavy lifting for you. He is the one who is going to help you begin to live free.

But as we go, you have one job to do. There is a second half to Galatians 5:1. Let's read it again: "It is for freedom that Christ has set us free. Stand firm, then, and do not let yourselves be burdened again by a yoke of slavery."

What did you notice? The verse says that if we want to walk in the freedom we've been given, it's our job to *stand firm*. And this standing firm is where the fight begins. For too long I and many people I know have sat back on our heels and dealt with depression and been attacked by anxiety. We've just taken it and assumed it was our lot in life. No more! Anxiety and depression will attack, but now we're going to learn how to attack back and fight for the freedom to which we've already been given access. We often see this in the Bible. In Joshua chapter 1, God promised that he was going to give Joshua what the Bible calls the promised land. God said it like this: "I will give you every place where you set your foot, as I promised Moses" (v. 3).

What Joshua didn't know was that he and the Israelites were going to have to fight thirty-one battles to take possession of the land that God had already set aside for them to possess.

God was teaching the nation of Israel then, and us today, that often he will give us things in this life, equip us for battle, and then expect us to go fight and take possession of the very things he's made possible for us to experience. Paul writes in Galatians 5 that God promised us Jesus has already bought our freedom. And now it's up to you and me to fight and take hold of that freedom. That's why, when anxiety and depression attack, we attack back!

The purpose of this book is to teach you how to do exactly that. I will show you how to use the God-given weapons at your disposal to take possession of the peace, joy, freedom, and confidence God wants you to experience—and I'm telling you this is possible for you today.

In part 1, I share three truths you need to know right off the bat. Then, once we lay a foundation, it's time to get to work. Part 2 is about all the things you need to start doing to move forward. Part 3 is about the false beliefs and patterns you need to stop (your journey toward freedom is going to involve you walking away from some stuff). And because learning to live free is a lifelong process, full of ups and downs, part 4 is about the things you need to remember along the way. I've also included an appendix, Panic Attack Survival Guide, which will give you some extremely practical things to do if you are having a panic attack or trying to help a loved one who is.

Through my story, the hard lessons I've learned, and his timeless Word, I believe God wants to speak to you about your struggles, or the struggles of your friends and family. God is going to help you and your loved ones begin to stand, fight, and take hold of the very freedom Jesus died to provide for you.

We've been *set free*, but now it's time to *live free*.

And I can't wait.

Let's go!

# Part 1
# KNOW

# YOU ARE NOT CRAZY

When I pulled my truck over to the side of the road, I thought my life was over. But that's not how my story ended.

After my wife and friends got me back to my house and I started to calm down, I decided to get serious about learning how to live free.

Through several difficult conversations and prayers, Jill and I decided I needed to take some serious steps. I was tired of putting Band-Aids over these massive wounds in my soul; I needed to get professional help. So I stepped away from the church for five months and went through an incredibly challenging but helpful journey of counseling and therapy.

My first stop was to see one of my pastors in Alabama. Pastor Chris Hodges and his team of pastors, doctors, and counselors spent two intense weeks with me, but that was just the beginning. After that, I went to seven weeks of inpatient, anti–anxiety and depression counseling. It was one of the hardest and most humbling things I've ever had to do, and it was honestly just the start of my counseling. But I came out the other side a different man. Eventually, I even went back to work. And today, I'm not just surviving—I'm experiencing joy and freedom at levels I wouldn't have even dreamed possible.

I know you may not have the luxury of doing all of that, which is why I'm writing this book. I want to walk you through my journey from feeling panicked and afraid to being alive and free. Along the way, I'm going to share what I learned from two weeks in Alabama and seven weeks of intensive inpatient counseling. I'm also going to share some of the moments that literally changed my life. And instead of holding back, I'm going to tell you everything I can about my journey because I believe it is going to help you on yours. But before we talk about all those months of counseling and life lessons learned, let's start with a moment that happened when I got back.

After my hiatus I was nervous about getting back onstage. People were about to find out just how messed up the guy with the microphone really was, and I was worried about what they might say. Unfortunately, you can't really disappear for five months and then jump back in, pretending like nothing happened—so I took the opposite approach.

I shared *everything*.

We have this line we say at our church: "We are a bunch of imperfect people pursuing a perfect God."

I've said it in about every sermon since I can remember. And as you now know, I don't just say it because it sounds good; I say it because it's true.

But that doesn't mean sharing those stories from the stage was easy. Even though I hoped the church would respond with love and acceptance, my first weekend back was terrifying.

If you are a public speaker, you know how awkward it feels to jump back up onstage when you've taken a few months off. Couple that with the elephant in the room—that I'd been MIA for almost half a year—and I was nervous.

But I got through it.

I climbed onstage and stumbled my way through that first sermon, sharing everything going on in my life. I told the congregation the story about my panic attack on the highway, my fight with anxiety, and where I'd been the last several months.

And as predicted, the church responded with love and support.

By the end of it, my tank was empty. It was an incredible night, but it was also emotionally draining, and I was ready to just be home. But as I was walking to my truck, an amazing family from the church stopped me. They all had tears in their eyes. They were staring at me, trying to find words, until finally, the dad spoke up.

"Thank you for being so open and honest about your struggles with anxiety," he said as the tears ran down his face. Then he pointed to his teenage son. "My son deals with severe anxiety."

I locked eyes with the son, who just nodded in solidarity. I could tell he had a million questions to ask, but words were escaping him. So his dad chimed back in.

"Shawn, can you tell my son what he needs to know right now? Because he's feeling a lot of anxiety and having panic attacks."

There are some moments in life where it feels like God is speaking right through you. This was one of those moments. Without thinking, I told him three things: "You are not crazy. You are not alone. And this will end."

And then we all just stood there and cried together.

The words just popped out of my mouth, but they struck a chord with everyone, including me. Those were the words I wish someone had said to me when I was on the side of the highway, ready to end it. Those are the three things I didn't know, three things I couldn't see, and—if I'm honest—three things I didn't believe.

But they are true.

Before we go any further, we need to take some time to let those words sink in. The starting point for dealing with anxiety and depression is *knowing* these three things are true. That's what we are going to accomplish in part 1. Those are the words I needed to hear at my lowest moment. Those are the words that young man needed to hear that night. And those are the words you need to hear right now.

*Because they are true.*

No matter what level of anxiety or depression you are dealing with, no matter how long it has been or how hopeless you feel:

You are not crazy.

You are not alone.

And this will end.

## YOU ARE NOT CRAZY

Last week, a man sat in my office, shaking. He told me he was having panic attacks daily and didn't know what to do. He was clenching his fists, clenching his jaw, and just trying to breathe as he rocked back and forth.

"I'm sorry," he kept saying. "I just don't know what's wrong with me."

"Can I tell you the most important thing you need to know

right now?" I said, trying to get him to relax and breathe. *"You are not crazy."*

The man had been staring at the ground for several minutes, but his eyes quickly shot up. He stared at me. I could tell this was a meaningful moment, so I said it again.

"You are not crazy."

He kept staring at me as if begging me to repeat it. So, I said for a third time, "You are not crazy."

And he broke. His shoulders dropped. His fists unclenched. And he began to sob. "I've been feeling crazy this whole time. Like I'm just so wrong."

"I know the way you feel," I said. "I felt the same way. Trust me. You are not crazy."

You and your loved ones need to hear this right now as bad as my friend did that day. So take this in:

You are not crazy. You're extremely normal. You just happen to be dealing with something that most people have been afraid to talk about for too long. So let this set you free today: *you are not crazy.*

According to the Centers for Disease Control and Prevention (CDC), the leading national public health institute of the United States, "Mental illnesses are among the most common health conditions in the United States,"[2] and anxiety and depression fall into this category.

Let's stop for a moment and take that in.

Have you ever felt like you are losing your mind? Like you are going crazy?

If you are anything like me, you've felt that way more than you care to admit. Anxiety and depression have an odd way of making you feel like you are losing it.

Forget about those feelings for a moment.

Forget that you don't know a lot about mental health issues.

Forget that you feel insane at times because more people don't talk about their own mental health problems.

The truth is, *mental illnesses are among the most common health conditions in the United States.*

You may feel like you are losing your mind, but *you are not crazy.*

You're not insane.

You're not on an island, experiencing something that nobody else is going through. You're not messed up in ways nobody else will understand. You're just a broken human like the rest of us.

We all have struggles, issues, habits, sin problems, and insecurities. We all deal with pain, heartache, illness, loneliness, and other difficult emotions.

We're all broken.

We're just broken differently.

Picture a baseball being thrown through a window and shattering it into eight billion pieces of glass. (It's a big window.) Imagine all those pieces falling to the ground, each one a different size and shape. That's us—all broken in different ways.

Stop seeing yourself as a freak, an outcast, or a misfit and take a second to see yourself as a child of God. You are a child of God, just like the rest of us. You are slightly broken, just like the rest of us.

You are normal.

Not crazy.

You've probably heard the phrase "misery loves company." I think the reason that statement rings true is because sometimes we just want to know that somebody else hurts like we hurt. We want to know that somebody else feels what we feel and deals with what we deal with. Because if we're not the only ones, then maybe we're not crazy. That's why I'm sharing all these stories—not because I enjoy the process but because I want you to know that I'm in this with you. And none of us are crazy.

———

After my panic attack on the highway that day, I figured I was losing my mind. It took five months of extremely difficult work for me to know (and I mean really *know*) that I was not the only one struggling with mental health issues. The most intense part of those five months was the seven-week, out-of-state, inpatient counseling. It was nonstop classes, counseling, and therapy. Six days a week for seven straight weeks. I think I've had more training than most counselors in my city. And from the other side of that experience, I now know beyond a shadow of a doubt that I am not crazy.

Through all that work, we discovered that my anxiety stems from four different places. To keep the transparency going, I want to walk you through all four areas. Because even though your story isn't going to match up exactly with mine, I know enough by now to know there is always overlap.

### Area #1: Past Abuse

Past abuse was the starting point for me.

Throughout my life, I've experienced emotional, physical, and sexual abuse. The details of my experiences with each of those aren't important, but if you have abuse in your past, there's a good chance it's feeding into your anxiety today. No matter how many years ago it was and how "over it" you may think you are, abuse causes wounds deep in your soul.

I went decades thinking I was over it.

After all, I was a grown man. I was a husband, a father, a lead pastor. Surely somewhere along the way, I'd managed to get over my abuse, right? In reality, I was just pretending. At times I convinced myself it hadn't happened. At other times I minimized the effects it had on me.

Both approaches are toxic.

Both cause our bodies and minds to hold on to past hurts.

And both feed into our anxieties.

In his fantastic book *The Body Keeps the Score*, Bessel van der Kolk says it this way: "As long as you keep secrets and suppress information, you are fundamentally at war with yourself. . . . The critical issue is allowing yourself to know what you know. That takes an enormous amount of courage."[3] Explaining how mental suppression impacts the body is well beyond the scope of my book, but I'd encourage you to check out his work if you are ready to take a deeper dive.

If you are on edge while reading this section, consider talking to a professional. Seriously. Forget about any stigma on counseling. Getting help was a game changer for me. It helped me acknowledge the effects abuse had on me, and it can do the same for you.

### Area #2: Current Pressures

Pressure was the second thing adding to my anxiety.

You can certainly relate to that one, can't you? Pressure is a part of life. It's something we all have to deal with. And it actually isn't a bad thing.

During one of my sessions, a counselor explained it to me in a way that I found super helpful. Without getting too deep into the psychology of this, essentially there are two types of anxiety:

1. *Facilitating anxiety* (healthy fear)
2. *Debilitating anxiety* (unhealthy fear)

Facilitating anxiety is good, healthy, and God-given. There is a reason you'd feel uncomfortable if you drove a hundred miles per hour down a long, dark country road or too close to the edge of a cliff.

It's because that's dangerous.

We should feel uncomfortable. That's God telling us to stop being dumb. He's got plans and a purpose for your life, and he's trying to keep you alive so that you can step into those things.

Facilitating anxiety also keeps you on your toes. I live in Colorado, and if I'm hiking up in the mountains with my boys at a certain time of year, we know there could be rattlesnakes on the path. It's good that we feel a bit on edge. Facilitating anxiety keeps us aware—it keeps us sharp.

Anytime you need to perform at your peak level, you should feel a little nervous energy. That energy puts us on high alert so we can perform.

Athletes should have some jitters before a big game. That's their bodies keeping them sharp. Businesspeople should need to take a few deep breaths before a big presentation or when they are trying to close a deal, make a sale, or take a challenge head-on.

Before I preach, I always get butterflies. When I'm about to walk onto a stage and speak in front of thousands of people, I need those butterflies. They help arouse my senses and keep me focused and energetic.

Facilitating anxiety is God's grace—it's a healthy fear.

But it's easy to let that fear go too far, isn't it?

When facilitating anxiety turns into debilitating anxiety, it begins to prohibit us from living our normal lives, doing our daily activities, and walking in God's calling. Debilitating anxiety is an unhealthy fear that causes us to stop living and enjoying our lives.

That's what happened to me.

The pressure got too high. I would preach a sermon, but then I'd get offstage and feel like I couldn't flip off the switch. It was stuck in the on position, and it was tearing apart my life.

It took several in-depth conversations with my wife, friends, pastors, counselors, and God to see it, acknowledge it, and begin to change.

Those conversations helped me reprioritize my life.

The first thing I had to do was learn the art of saying no. Did you know you are allowed to say that? Seriously. You can't be all things to all people. I was trying to be. And because of that, I was running out of time for the most important people in my life.

I started guarding my time for the things I knew I really needed to do. I got very intentional about creating a rhythm in my life that allows me to work hard, rest when necessary, and spend my best hours doing what's most important to me, like making time with my family a priority.

If you are trying to figure out where to start on your journey toward shedding current pressures and decreasing debilitating anxiety, try this simple exercise: Write out the things you spend your hours doing on a typical weekday. Jot down everything you can think of, from meetings to your commute to who you spend the most time with. Then, on a separate piece of paper, write out the things in life that are most important to you.

When you hold those two pieces of paper up next to each other, the contrast will be very revealing (and probably a little painful). But I promise it will be helpful.

It will show you the things in your life you need to keep and the things you need to begin weeding out. That will make it easier to start saying no to *good* things so that you have more time for *great* things.

Before long, you will find yourself with way more space. You'll begin operating with more peace and less frantic, anxiety-ridden activity.

### Area #3: Self-Inflicted Pressures

The next demon I had to face was all the self-inflicted pressure I was putting on myself—pressure on myself that God never intended for me to carry. I was performing for everyone in my life, thinking I needed to perform for the love and acceptance of my wife, family, kids, and even God.

In my career, I was comparing myself to the best in the world. Thanks to social media, I would watch my sixty-second highlight reel from the weekend, then scroll down and see the clips from the guys who were doing what I was trying to do in the way I wished I could do it.

It was an endless loop of comparison.

And it was exhausting.

We'll get into this later, but I realized that either that mindset had to die or it was going to kill me. I was experiencing the culmination of several years of self-induced pressure that said, *You'd better keep performing if you want anyone, especially God, to love and stay with you.* Nothing could have been further from the truth, but that's what I believed.

And I bet I'm not the only one who has believed these lies.

### Area #4: Chemical Imbalance

It's a simple fact that many people, including me, have some things going on in our brains that make us more susceptible to anxiety and depression.

Getting on appropriate medication for a proper amount of time has been huge for me. But I'm not a doctor, so find yourself one who has experience in this area. Find someone who will take the time to listen to you and get to know your situation, then see if they think that medication is a good idea.

# WHAT ABOUT YOU?

I realize that was very brief. Don't worry. As we go along, I'll get into the deep weeds and share with you the most valuable lessons I've learned while dealing with anxiety and depression in all four of those areas.

The purpose of this section is not to counsel you through each of these based on your experiences but to serve as a reminder that *you are not crazy.* This stuff is real and way more common than you may have known.

If you deal with mental illness, hopefully this is already beginning to feel cathartic and freeing.

Other people deal with this too.

You can exhale.

You are not crazy!

# FOR ME

Here's one of the most common questions people ask me: "So, what's it like for you?"

Some people who ask me that question don't struggle with anxiety or depression; they are honestly just curious. But when most people ask, I can tell they are hoping I'll say something that sounds even remotely similar to what they are going through. I can see it in their eyes; they just want to know they aren't crazy.

*Maybe I'm not crazy.*

*Maybe there is someone else who knows how I feel.*

*Maybe, just maybe, it's not just me.*

So, since we've already come this far, how about I tell you exactly what I feel and think when I'm at my worst. I'm going to share (in detail, like I did in the introduction) what goes through my head when it gets real bad. Not because I like humiliating myself but because I'm tired of this lie the Enemy tries to tell us, that we are crazy. I bought into it for too long; now I'm on a mission to let the world know they are not crazy.

Revelation 12:11 says two things defeat the power of Satan in someone's life: "They triumphed over him by the blood of the Lamb and by the word of their testimony."

I love how simple that two-step process is.

Jesus died on the cross to pay the price for our sins. He did his part. Now it's time for me to do my part. Our job is to share with one another the stories of how far God has brought us.

So here goes.

## Anxiety

When I'm feeling anxious, my mind and my body both react. And both seem to make the other worse. First, my mind starts spinning, and I panic because I know what's coming. Then my skin starts to crawl and my chest tightens. But that puts my mind on high alert, and I begin to think, *Here it comes. You aren't going to be able to stop it once it starts.*

This makes my breath get even shorter, my chest get even tighter, and my skin start tingling everywhere.

*Yep, this is it,* I think. *This one is going to be even worse.*

Then my body goes to a whole other level. I feel out of control. Trapped. Stuck. And scared it will never end. And no matter where I'm at or who is around, all I want to do is escape.

*I'm going to suffocate.*

*I can't get enough air.*

*This space isn't big enough.*

So I start hyperventilating, which doesn't help my cause at all. And that's about the time the lies set in.

*I'm crazy.*

*I'm wrong.*

*Nobody will understand.*

*I can't live this way.*

*I have to escape.*

*I can't.*

That's when I start taking off seat belts, rolling down windows, getting off airplanes, leaving dinners, missing parties, ditching celebrations, and bailing on family functions.

Because all I know is I have to get out of there.

Simultaneously, I fixate on who is watching, wondering if any of them go to my church and thinking about how stupid I must look.

The thought that I can't escape is overwhelming. I become convinced that if I don't get out of whatever I'm doing, it will never end. I will surely die.

I walk out. I leave. I pull my car over. I avoid places where it might happen. And worse, I live in constant fear that it might happen again.

What I just described can happen in a nanosecond, and it's just the beginning of the agony of dealing with full-fledged anxiety attacks.

## Depression

When I'm depressed, I feel it more in my gut than my chest.

It starts as a pit in my stomach that makes breathing a little bit harder. It feels heavy and dark. In the middle of a bad day of depression when I was trying to explain it to my wife, I once said, "My heart feels black." That darkness and heaviness are somehow connected from my body to my brain, so all my mind does is focus on negative things.

It begins instantly lying to me, saying things like:

- *You can't.*
- *You won't.*
- *Nobody will care.*
- *Nobody does care.*

- *You are worthless.*
- *It wouldn't matter if you tried.*

I become overwhelmed with this lethargic feeling. It's heavy. It's dark. It's lonely. It's isolating. It's paralyzing.

I don't want to get up. I don't want to move. I don't want to eat. And if I do, I'll eat horribly and then feel worse after. And as people who love me or interact with me on a consistent basis look at me, I know they can see it, and I know they don't get it, and I know I can't explain it, and all of that makes me want to just disappear.

*I'm pathetic. I know it. I know you can see it. I'd change it if I could. But I can't.*

And that's just the beginning of depression for me. Sometimes it lasts for minutes. Other times it could last for days.

## The Perfect Storm

And every now and then, the combination of anxiety and depression turns into a feeling of hopelessness and even suicidal thoughts. Satan whispers lies in my ear. I believe lies on my own. And the combination of the two gets me thinking things like:

- *This world might be better off without me.*
- *The people who I love might be better off without me.*
- *I'll never get better.*
- *I'll never be right.*
- *I'll never be fixed.*
- *I'm always going to hurt.*
- *No one will ever understand.*
- *I'm making life worse for the people I work with.*

- *I'm making life harder for the people who love me.*
- *This world would be better off without me.*

# KEEP GOING

Well, that got heavy quick.

Yep.

That's how anxiety and depression work. They come out of nowhere and hit harder than you ever imagined. It's not just you.

You are not crazy.

Broken? Sure.

A work in progress? Of course.

Just like everyone else in the world. Join the party. You, me, and every other living soul are in the same boat.

And here's the fantastic news: your healing can begin right now, at this moment. Remember, my testimony is *not* just the part about being overwhelmed; it's also about being set free from this stuff in ways I never dreamed possible. I'm not perfect, not even close. But I'm also not where I used to be. I'm stronger, healthier, and better than I was in ways I didn't think I'd ever be. And I believe the same can be true for you and your loved ones.

All you have to do is run to God.

You don't have to be embarrassed about your brokenness or humiliated by your emotions. God already knows all your thoughts and actions anyway, yet he still invites us to come to him. "Let us then approach God's throne of grace with confidence, so that we may receive mercy and find grace to help us in our time of need" (Hebrews 4:16).

You are a child of God.

He loves you just the way you are.

He wants you to come to him in your "time of need."

When you're at your lowest.

When you hit bottom.

When you feel wrong and messy and broken.

The Bible says "our time of need" is the very moment God invites us to run to him to receive his mercy, grace, and help.

For some, that moment is right now. If this chapter stirred some things up in you that you've been trying to push down, this is your moment. You don't have to clean yourself up before you approach God; you can approach God with confidence right in the middle of your darkest time.

You haven't shocked God.

Your life may feel like it is unraveling, but I promise you God can help put it back together. Let's run to him. Let's go to the throne of grace boldly, and let's watch God do some incredible things in our lives.

*You are not crazy.*

You are not alone.

And this will end.

# YOU ARE NOT ALONE

If you ask anyone who has been to prison what the worst punishment is, they will tell you solitary confinement is the absolute worst thing you could ever experience.

It's torture.

And I don't need to explain that to you, do I? We don't need to experience solitary confinement to know how bad it is; there is something inside all of us that knows we were not created to live in isolation. Check out the first critique (observation) God had of creation at the beginning of the Bible: "It is not good for the man to be alone" (Genesis 2:18).

Every single one of us was created to pursue the plans of God with the people of God. Scripture tells us to "rejoice with those who rejoice; mourn with those who mourn" (Romans 12:15). God built us to celebrate the highs and battle through the lows together.

We were created for community!

One of the reasons mental illness is so dangerous is because it tends to isolate us. Anxiety and depression feed us the lie that we are the only ones struggling, and if you are anything like me, you start to believe it. We become convinced not only that we are crazy but also that no one will ever understand. And so, instead of talking about it, we check ourselves into our own self-prescribed solitary confinement.

Sound familiar?

If you have a loved one who deals with this, odds are you've watched them go down the destructive path toward isolation. And I'd imagine it was incredibly frustrating. If you've ever tried to console them, there is a good chance you've felt invisible. Let me speak for them, and please hear me: that is nothing personal. It has nothing to do with you.

*I am alone.*

During panic attacks, I have literally uttered those words right to my wife's face. Obviously, that is a very hurtful thing to say to the person sitting next to me, helping me weather the storm. The problem is, when we are going through severe anxiety and depression, there is a loudspeaker in our heads shouting:

- *You are crazy.*
- *You are alone.*
- *Don't you dare share what you're going through.*
- *Everyone will let you down.*
- *Everyone will lose respect for you.*
- *No one will understand.*
- *They might even leave you.*
- *Things will never get better.*
- *Things will only get worse.*

We don't want to push people away, but eventually the loud voice wears us down and convinces us not to share the depths of our pain with anyone. The more we believe the lie, the more we will be tempted to keep the depths of our anxiety and depression to ourselves.

We'll struggle in isolation while our loved ones sit right next to us, frustrated that they can't check us out of our self-prescribed solitary confinement. By the way, I know how scary it can be to have a panic attack and how frustrating it can feel to want to help a loved one but not know what to do or say. So at the back of this book, there is an appendix called the "Panic Attack Survival Guide." It will give you five things to do if you are having an attack and five things to do if you are trying to help someone you love through an attack.

Whether you struggle with anxiety and depression or love someone who does, the second thing you have to know is that *you are not alone.*

Seriously.

The thought that you are alone is a lie from the pit of hell.

If you deal with anxiety or depression, you're not even in the minority. But don't take my word for it; let's look at what the professionals, the church, and the Bible have to say.

## THE PROFESSIONALS

Let's hear from the CDC again:

> Problems with mental health are very common in the United
> States, with an estimated 50% of all Americans diagnosed with

a mental illness or disorder at some point in their lifetime. Mental illnesses, such as depression, are the third most common cause of hospitalization in the United States for those aged 18–44 years old.[4]

Did you catch that?

An estimated 50 percent. That means everywhere you go, whatever room you walk into, whatever coffee shop you are currently reading this book in, you are surrounded by people who share your struggle. The people you see every day at your school, work, neighborhood, and even in your own family are right there with you.

You are not alone.

# THE CHURCH

Sometimes Sunday morning can be a very isolating experience. It's easy to look around and believe the lie that you are the only one struggling. You see everyone raising hands in worship while you are stuck in your own personal hell, feeling like you don't belong. But nothing could be further from the truth.

We recently polled thousands of people at our church and asked them which topics they'd like to hear talked about. Take a wild guess at what made the top of the list: anxiety and depression. Why? Because everyone is either in the middle of dealing with these things or knows someone who is.

When I saw the results, I remember feeling two strong emotions. The first was pain; it hurt my soul to think about how many people are struggling. But I was also incredibly proud of our church for stepping up and being honest. We should be leading the way in this conversation. Gone are the days of pretending like we have it all together; it's time for the church to talk about anxiety and depression. Because as it turns out, even some of the greatest names in the Bible, heroes of the faith, fought the same battle and were courageous enough to admit it.

You are not alone!

# THE BIBLE

One of the many things I love about the Bible is its authenticity. God could have painted a picture of the heroes of our faith as being perfect, always mentally and emotionally strong and confident, but he didn't. He showed us their strengths, their weaknesses, their victories, and their failures. And most importantly for us in this context, we catch a glimpse of their very real inner struggles. As you're about to see, some of the most influential individuals to walk the face of this earth dealt with anxiety, depression, and mental and emotional anguish—just like we do. It's so freeing when we begin to truly understand that we, and those we love, are not alone in this. As you read this section, let that really begin to sink in: It's not just you; it's not just your loved ones. You are not alone!

## The Apostle Paul

Let's start with Paul, one of the most influential Christians to ever live. The man who wrote nearly half the books in the New Testament and took the gospel further than anyone before him. The guy who planted churches all around the known world. Listen to what he said to some of his friends who lived in a city called

Corinth: "We do not want you to be uninformed, brothers and sisters, about the troubles we experienced in the province of Asia. We were under great pressure, far beyond our ability to endure, so that we *despaired of life itself*" (2 Corinthians 1:8, emphasis added).

Those are big words. Life's pressures were more than he could handle. At some point, he didn't feel like he could keep going. By the way, he was writing this letter to a church that he started. Leaders, please listen to me. Paul was the guy everyone was looking to, and yet he was courageous enough to admit he was dealing with so much anxiety, depression, and hopelessness that he had moments where he "despaired of life itself." If he could say it, so can we!

The apostle Paul dealt with anxiety and depression. Let that encourage you. You don't have to hide it or be embarrassed, and you certainly aren't too weak to be used by God.

You are not alone.

### King David

Remember David? The one who killed Goliath with a slingshot and later became the greatest king Israel ever had? The one God called "a man after my own heart" (Acts 13:22)? Well, that mighty man of God also wrote this: "Why, my soul, are you downcast? Why so disturbed within me?" (Psalm 42:5).

What a great way to describe anxiety and depression. Notice in one verse David described dealing with both at the same time. His soul was both downcast *and* disturbed because the two go hand in hand. David had the courage to stand up and admit he wasn't okay.

This wasn't a mild case either; the next time you have your Bible open, read the rest of Psalm 42. David didn't think he was going to make it. He was not eating, he couldn't stop crying, and he couldn't handle how disturbed he was on the inside. If you know anxiety and depression, these feelings are all too familiar. David wasn't embarrassed by his emotional state, and we shouldn't be either.

You are not alone.

## Jesus

Not to beat a dead horse, but if it makes you feel any better, Jesus knows how you feel. Listen to what he said in Matthew 26:36–38:

> Then Jesus went with his disciples to a place called Gethsemane,
> and he said to them, "Sit here while I go over there and pray."
> He took Peter and the two sons of Zebedee along with him, and
> he began to be sorrowful and troubled. Then he said to them,
> "My soul is overwhelmed with sorrow to the point of death.
> Stay here and keep watch with me."

This was Jesus—God in the form of a man. And he understood what it was like to be so overwhelmed with sorrow that it felt like death. It's no wonder the writer of Hebrews told us, "For we do not have a high priest who is unable to empathize with our weaknesses, but we have one who has been tempted in every way, just as we are—yet he did not sin" (4:15).

Listen, you are not the only one. Do you believe me yet? The thing is, you can hear what the professionals say, listen to the cry of the masses at church, read about the heroes of the faith, even hear the truth from Jesus himself, and *still feel alone.*

On paper, that makes absolutely no sense, yet that's been the experience for so many of us. What's the problem? How come, despite the overwhelming evidence, we still feel alone?

Whether you know it or not, there is a spiritual battle going on right now for your soul, your freedom, and your ability to live free.

## The Thief

There is an Enemy whispering lies into your ear, trying to drag you back down into isolation. Jesus said it best: "The thief comes only to steal and kill and destroy; I have come that they may have life, and have it to the full" (John 10:10).

Jesus came to this earth to go to the cross, pay for our sins, and make a way for us to live free. But Satan is very real, and he wants to steal, kill, and destroy every good thing in your life. He wants to rob you of the very freedom Jesus died to provide you with, and Satan has one very predictable yet deceptive tactic.

Satan doesn't just tell lies; he is a liar. The Bible calls him "the father of lies" (John 8:44). If you are keeping track at home, so far he's been called a thief and the father of lies. How's that for a rap sheet? Remember, his goal is to get in your head and steal away all your hope, and he does so by whispering lies to convince you you're all by yourself. You've heard these lies before, haven't you?

- *I'm a mom. I'm not supposed to struggle like this.*
- *I'm a dad. My family needs me to be stronger than this.*
- *I'm a supervisor. I should have it more together.*
- *I'm a CEO. My emotions shouldn't be this unpredictable.*
- *Leaders aren't supposed to be weak.*
- *If these people find out how much I struggle, they'll leave.*
- *I gave my life to God. I'm not supposed to struggle still.*
- *I volunteer at my church. I shouldn't be feeling this way.*

The list goes on and on. Trust me, I know the feeling. Here's how it usually plays out for me: *I'm a pastor. I work at a church full-time. I talk about God for a living. I shouldn't still be dealing with this. It's just me. Surely, nobody at my stage of life, with the blessings I've been given, has anxiety and depression.*

Do you see the move? Satan's lies always move us toward isolation. He wants you to keep everything in the dark, so his tactic is to make you feel like you are alone.

To quote my friend Levi Lusko:

> Darkness is dangerous. Anything in your life that you are trying to keep a secret, hidden in the dark, is holding you back and will harm you eventually. Think about it. Nothing healthy grows in the dark. Flowers, trees, fruits, and vegetables—the kind of things that you want to grow—they all require sunshine. Mold spores, fungi, moss, these are the kinds of things that thrive in dark environments. The kind of growth you don't want is what you will find in secret, shady places.[5]

That haunting picture perfectly describes my former situation. I kept my pain in the dark, hoping it would disappear, wondering where all this anxiety and depression was coming from.

Believe me, I was trying to speak up. Before people knew how bad it was, I would start trying to talk, but Satan knew that would lead to freedom, so he'd jump in and tell me lies:

- *They won't understand me.*
- *They'll never see me the same.*
- *They won't trust me.*
- *They won't respect me.*

- *They might not love me.*
- *They've got their own issues in life to deal with—they don't need mine on top of that.*

The voices were just too loud and too persuasive, so I'd stuff my struggle down and keep it to myself for the rest of the day. But one day turned into one week, which turned into a month, which turned into several years. I blinked, and before I knew it, I was sobbing on the side of the highway, spiraling out of control, wondering if I could keep on living, and the people closest to me didn't even know how bad it really was.

That's solitary confinement.

That's torture.

And I get it. It feels real.

But it's a lie.

# INTO THE LIGHT

Do you know what's wild?

Once it all came out; once my wife, friends, and coworkers heard the struggle straight from my lips; once I told them how bad it was—they all respected me more, and they were able to love me even more authentically. It brought us all closer together because they knew how to help fight with me. Talking about your struggles is like shining a bright light on them, but Satan had sold me on the idea that I needed to keep my struggles to myself or else I would lose all my authority and respect as a Christian leader. Nothing could have been further from the truth. My honesty brought a brand-new level of freedom.

God meant what he said:

> Two are better than one,
>> because they have a good return for their labor:
> If either of them falls down,
>> one can help the other up.
> But pity anyone who falls
>> and has no one to help them up. . . .
> Though one may be overpowered,
>> two can defend themselves.
> A cord of three strands is not quickly broken.
>> (Ecclesiastes 4:9–10, 12)

The father of lies is trying to keep us all in isolation. And I'm tired of it. So I'm calling it out. He's lying to you. The thief has been stealing your peace, killing your joy, and destroying your hope for too long. It's time to put an end to it. It's time to attack back! And our offensive battle plan starts with real, honest conversation with people we love and trust.

## BREAK THE SILENCE

One of the biggest lies I bought into was that silence was a viable solution. Somewhere in the recesses of my mind, the Enemy convinced me that I should keep my mouth shut. But I was wrong. The truth is:

- I needed a counselor to help start to untangle the mess.
- I needed therapy to deal with my past pain and trauma.

- I needed to let my wife in on everything.
- I needed my kids to walk with me.
- I needed my friends to fight alongside me.

What's worse is my counselor, therapist, wife, kids, and friends all wanted and were ready to help. But I missed out on all of it for so long because I was too afraid, prideful, ashamed, and embarrassed to break the silence.

I want to invite you to join me. Fear kept me in the dark, and I don't want you to make the same mistake. If you struggle with anxiety or depression, have an honest conversation with someone you love and trust, or maybe even talk to a counselor. Just admit that your struggle is there so you can begin processing it in some God-given ways.

If you struggle with anxiety or depression, you aren't crazy; you are just broken like the rest of us. Welcome to the party! Talk about it with someone. There is so much freedom in verbalizing it out loud. If you keep it in the dark, it will grow, but as soon as you bring it to the light, it will lose so much of its power.

## THE GOD OF HOPE

I know this is a lot to take in, but remember, we have a God of *hope* who plans to fill you with joy and peace. Let this verse speak to you today. Let the God of the universe breathe life and encouragement into you right now: "May the God of hope fill you with all joy and peace as you trust in him, so that you may overflow with hope by the power of the Holy Spirit" (Romans 15:13).

This battle can feel hopeless at times. Trust me; I know the feeling. But despite how we may *feel*, the *fact* is God can completely replace that hopelessness with an overflowing hope. He is going to do it. And it won't be because you magically became strong enough to defeat the Enemy on your own; it will be because *his power* is at work in you.

You can do this! Your God is at work. Remember these three things as we begin the journey toward freedom:

1. You are not crazy.
2. You are not alone.
3. This will end.

# THIS WILL END

I love a good action movie.

Especially one where the hero defies the odds and overcomes seemingly impossible obstacles. If you are anything like me, something in your soul comes alive when you watch a movie like that.

The thing about every heroic comeback story is that they all start the same way. In fact, they all follow the same formula: the hero hits rock bottom, and all hope seems lost, but just when it looks like things can't get worse, the hero turns the situation around and emerges victorious.

Think about the beginning of every Marvel movie. The hero goes through something tragic, and we are left to wonder how he or she will ever bounce back. Harry Potter loses his parents before chapter 1 and has to live under the stairs at his evil aunt and uncle's house. Each Star Wars movie begins with the evil empire in control, and this time around, there is no way the good guys will be able to stop it. And, of course, every Tom Cruise movie starts with a mission that, in fact, feels impossible.

On and on we could go. In order for there to be a compelling comeback, there first has to be a deficit. If you are writing a screenplay, here's a good formula to remember: *the greater the deficit, the better the comeback.*

What does all that have to do with anxiety and depression?

Well, comeback stories aren't just for the big screen; they are true about our everyday lives. God is in the business of writing comeback stories in and through our lives.

Have you ever noticed that the word *testimony* (the story of what God has done in your life) begins with the word *test*?

Right now, you may feel like your situation is impossible. Your mental health may make you want to give up or throw in the towel. You may be so consumed in a season of anxiety and depression that you can't possibly imagine a brighter future, but that's a lie. You need to know that. What if all the obstacles you are facing are simply setting the scene for a fantastic story?

Put simply: *the greater the test, the greater the testimony.*

If that feels impossible to you, here's the really good news: that's okay. It's better than okay. That's the setup for the perfect comeback story.

Impossible is God's specialty!

And I'm telling you, you will pull through this, and you're going to have a life-changing story to share with others one day that will blow you away. In the next section, we will dive into some of the tangible steps we need to start taking. But first, there is one last truth you need to know.

Please hear me: this *will* end!

# THE IMPOSSIBLE AND THE POSSIBLE

One day, Jesus looked at a group of people and said something so profound that Matthew decided to include it in his gospel. And thank God he did because it's something I often need to hear. "With man this is impossible, but with God all things are possible" (Matthew 19:26).

All things are possible with God.

Picture your anxiety.

Picture your depression.

Picture the level of hopelessness you've felt at your lowest point.

Got it?

Okay, now picture the God of the universe who knows you better than anyone on this planet, the God who knows exactly what you've been through and precisely what you are facing. Hear him saying this to you: *with me, nothing is impossible.*

That's what God is telling you today. *This is not the end.* This is not how your story is going to finish. I believe God wants you to begin to understand that right now. Today, as bad as things can look and feel, God's just getting started in your life.

With him, all things are possible!

The fact that I'm alive and able to write about mental health today is a miracle. I'm serious. It's proof in and of itself that our God is still in the miracle-working and life-changing business.

I gave up that day on the side of the road.

I quit my job.

I gave away my guns because I was worried about what I might do.

I convinced myself that my family, friends, and church would be better off without me.

And honestly, I hadn't even hit rock bottom yet (more on that later).

What I needed to know that day is the same thing you or maybe your loved one needs to know right now.

This is not the end.

Listen to what the Word of God has to say about your life: "Being confident of this, that he who began a good work in you will carry it on to completion until the day of Christ Jesus" (Philippians 1:6).

God finishes what he starts.

Believe it or not, God has begun a work in your life that he *will* bring to completion. God's not going to just get you or your loved one through this season; he's building a testimony that can change the world around you for the rest of your life. And remember, the greater the *test*, the greater the *testimony*.

Don't you dare give up!

If you look up any great success story, they all have one thing in common: the situation looked hopeless, and then something amazing happened. That's how our God works. This is what God does. He picks us up at our lowest points and takes us to heights greater than anything we could think of or imagine.

And he is about to blow everyone away with the amazing things he is going to do in and through your life, or through the life of that person you care about who is struggling.

This is the pattern throughout Scripture. Think about any of your favorite Bible heroes—the ones who did something amazing. They had a time in the wilderness before they started seeing victory in their lives.

It's the same pattern as all our favorite movies: something

went wrong, Satan tried to take them out, and then God came in, turned it around, and used all the bad for good.

God loves to show off!

He loves to take broken and desperate situations and turn them into something beautiful. Let's take a look at a few examples.

# ABRAHAM

God gave Abraham (Father Abraham if you grew up singing in Sunday school) a big dream. God declared that Abraham was going to start the nation of Israel. The only problem was, Abraham didn't have any kids. I'm not the smartest guy in the world, but I know enough to know you can't be the father of an entire nation if you don't even have your first kid.

To make matters worse, Abraham was nearly one hundred years old at the time, and his wife wasn't much younger, plus she was barren. They had tried for years and hadn't had any luck. Things couldn't have looked grimmer.

*But the greater the test, the greater the testimony.*

God intervened and did the impossible. Abraham and his wife conceived and had a son, and the nation of Israel was off to the races.

Abraham probably thought his story was over, but God knew the truth; Father Abraham was just getting started.

# JOSEPH

Abraham's great-grandson Joseph had a dream of being a leader. He was positive God had placed that dream on his heart. He didn't know exactly what it was going to look like, but he knew he was going to lead people, help people, and make a difference in the world. Just like you right now, Joseph knew God had a plan for his life.

However, the day his own brothers beat him up and threw him into a pit, I'd imagine he thought his dream was over. When he was dragged off to a foreign land to be a slave, he surely thought his dream was over. When he was thrown into an Egyptian prison for a crime he hadn't even committed—he must have thought his dream was over.

*But the greater the test, the greater the testimony.*

God intervened and did the impossible, and Joseph ended up saving a nation (and his entire family) from a severe famine. He thought his story was done, but God was just getting started. Don't gloss over this. Joseph's journey may have had low points, but at the end of the day, he saved an entire nation.

When he faced his trials, he needed to know the same thing you need to know today: *Your story is not over. Not even close. God is just getting started!*

# MOSES

Moses had a dream of being used by God in big ways, but for the majority of his life, things didn't seem like they were going as planned. When he was forty years old, he committed murder, got scared, and ran for his life. By the time he was nearing eighty, he was still out in the middle of nowhere, watching someone else's sheep in a field.

At that point, I assume he had probably thrown the towel in and just thought his life would end in obscurity.

*But the greater the test, the greater the testimony.*

Even if you've never been to church, you've probably heard of Moses, haven't you? That's because his story didn't end in hopelessness or obscurity. He saved the entire nation of Israel from the most powerful empire on the planet. He watched as God parted the sea, and he led what some scholars believe to be upward of two million people through it. He became one of the most influential men to walk on this planet.

How was that possible?

God intervened and did the impossible.

Moses probably thought his story was over, but God knew the truth; Moses was just getting started.

# THE DISCIPLES

I promise this will be the last biblical comparison. We'll move on after this one, but before we do, we have to talk about the Friday night after Jesus was crucified on the cross to pay the price for our sins.

When his body was placed in a tomb, all the disciples (and every other Jesus follower on the planet) must've lost hope. Remember, we have the luxury of knowing the end of the story, but they had no idea. They would've been absolutely convinced their story was done.

The disciples thought their story was over, but God knew the truth; he was just getting started.

They learned something that Sunday morning as Jesus miraculously walked out of the tomb. Often, when we think we've hit the absolute bottom, when we think we are at the end, we realize God has been working behind the scenes the entire time.

What we call the end, God calls the start of something brand new.

I need you to see this about your life right now. I need you to see this about the life of your loved one who is struggling right now.

The anxiety.

The depression.

The hopelessness.

I know how overwhelming it all feels. But this is not the end of your story. God is at work. He does the impossible. And I'm telling you, he is just getting started.

## ROCK BOTTOM

After I pulled the car over to the side of the road and spent two weeks with my pastor in Alabama, I headed off for seven weeks of inpatient, anti–anxiety and depression counseling. Remember when I told you earlier that I thought I had hit rock bottom on the side of the road? I realized one night in counseling that I had further down to go.

I hadn't hit rock bottom yet, but I would that night in counseling.

I was already in one of the worst funks of my entire life, and then some things happened in my personal and professional life that sent me into a spiral so deep that I didn't think I would make it out.

I lay on the floor that night for hours.

Crying.

Sobbing.

Shaking.

Snot was flying everywhere. It was ugly.

"It hurts so bad," was all I could say to my wife. I just said it over and over again. "It hurts so bad. It hurts so bad. It hurts so bad."

My mind convinced me not only that it was the end of my story but also that it was the end of my life. And in that moment, the greatest lies of depression and anxiety worked their way into my mind:

*The people in my life would be better off without me.*

*My boys can't see me this way.*

*My wife shouldn't have to see me this way.*

*My friends don't want to see me this way.*

*I can't let the people I pastor see me this way.*

I know how bad anxiety can hurt and depression can devastate. I know the lies that hopelessness tells us. But listen to me—those are lies from the pit of hell. I can see that now, but it felt so real in the moment. Please hear me: nobody in this world will be better off without you. If you decide to die by suicide because you think you're at the end, every single person who cares about you will live with an unreal pain for the rest of their lives. You will do so much more harm than good.

Let me say that again in case you have been listening to the lies of Satan—nobody in this world will be better off without you.

And I promise you, you're going to turn around one day and realize how far you've come since rock bottom. Things will get better. You will find a level of peace, joy, confidence, security, and hopefulness that you never thought possible. And at that moment, you will be so thankful that you didn't do anything stupid.

Don't you dare give up right now because this is not the end of your story.

I know because I've lived it.

The morning after I spent the night sobbing on the floor, telling my wife how bad it hurt, I called the CEO of the counseling facility I was enrolled in. Jill and I sat down with him, and I very calmly and very seriously explained that I was at rock bottom.

I said my mind was made up. I was 100 percent certain I was going to take my own life. I was meeting with them to figure out how we were going to help our three boys get through this.

With a clear mind (or so I thought) and all the emotion removed, I had decided this world would be better off without me—that was rock bottom.

If you feel like your anxiety and depression will never end, I understand. If your loved one feels like their depression, anxiety, and hopelessness will never end, I understand. But what I also understand is that those are lies. Nobody would have been better off without me. My counselors helped me see the truth when I couldn't see it for myself. My wife helped me see the truth when I couldn't see it for myself. Let me help you see it right now if you can't see it for yourself: this is not the end of your story. God has a plan for your life, and that plan includes levels of freedom you can't imagine. You can't see it yet, but you will.

With the help of outside voices of truth and reason, I continued to fight. I didn't give up. I didn't end up doing anything stupid or harmful to myself. In fact, I began attacking my anxiety with the very tools I'm going to share with you through the rest of this book. Today I find myself healthier, better, and stronger than I ever could have imagined—and I'm praying the same thing will be true for you and your loved ones.

This is not the end.

Again, I know this because I'm living proof. Don't you dare give up. I never thought my life would get better, and I never thought things would turn around. But today, I am sitting on a couch in my office right now writing to you, and I can tell you with 100 percent honesty that I am experiencing more peace, more joy, more hope, more confidence, and more faith in the future than I ever thought possible.

I am so thankful I never did anything stupid when my emotions were lying to me. God is working in your life right now, even if you can't see it. You will get better.

Our God is a God of:

- new mercies,
- new mornings,
- new starts,
- new beginnings,
- new creations.

Our God restores our lives, and he uses the trials we've been through to bring us more purpose than we ever thought possible.

In the next section, we are going to get super practical and begin talking about all the things we need to start doing to experience the freedom God's already promised us, but first, you need to know this is not the end. Your story and your life are not over. He has plans and a hope and a future in store for you that will absolutely blow you away.

Yes, you're in the middle of a test.

Yes, it feels impossible.

But yes, your God is at work. Don't you dare give up. God

is just getting started! And remember, the greater the test, the greater the testimony. You are going to win this battle, but first, you have to know:

1. You are not crazy.
2. You are not alone.
3. This will end.

# Part 2
## *START*

# FIGHTING

Waking up the morning after a breakdown is a strange experience. The next day after my roadside experience, I lay in my bed and tried to wrap my mind around everything that had happened.

My friends were gone.

My guns were gone.

My pride was gone.

And my wife was scared.

Since we were unsure what our next step should be, Jill decided to call Pastor Chris, who always seems to know the next right move. She told him what was going on, and without skipping a beat, he told her to get us on an airplane and come see him in Alabama.

Those were pretty simple instructions. For most people, that wouldn't have been a big deal. But for me, at the time, he might as well have told us to climb Mount Everest.

Claustrophobia is a huge part of my panic attacks. The thought of being in an enclosed plane, thirty thousand feet in the air, sounded less than ideal to me. I was in no state to fly, and my panic attacks were so frequent that I didn't feel like I stood a chance of getting through a day of traveling. I had a bad feeling about the trip from the start, but I had no idea just how bad it was going to be.

The first flight was from Denver to Dallas.

I was a little anxious, but with my wife sitting next to me, I got through it. The second flight was the problem. We boarded a plane from Dallas to Birmingham, and as soon as the doors closed, my anxiety started ramping up.

*I'm trapped.*

*I can't get out of here.*

*I need to get out of here.*

*I have no control.*

*This could last for hours.*

I kept trying to take deep breaths, but I felt like I couldn't breathe. Every time a flight attendant walked by, I just smiled and nodded, trying to appear as normal as I could. But the panic was ramping up.

As we taxied out on the runway, it got worse. At that point, sitting still was the last thing I wanted to do, which is a problem when the Fasten Seat Belts sign is on and the plane is on an active runway.

The flight attendant asked me to fasten my seat belt, but I couldn't bring myself to do it; I had to stand up. About that time, another flight attendant came over and asked me what was going on.

"I'm fine," I lied. "Really, I'm good. I'm just trying to breathe."

Since those two statements don't go together, she saw right through my charade. "Please take your seat, sir."

"I will in just a second," I said, probably looking like I'd lost my mind. "I just need a moment."

Then she walked away. For a second, I thought I had convinced her I was okay. But the next thing I knew, the airplane was leaving the runway and heading back to the gate. While a plane full of people groaned, they brought out that giant mechanical hallway, connected it back to the side of the aircraft, and opened the plane door. Then the pilot came out of the cockpit, walked up to me (in front of everyone), and told me I needed to get off the plane.

"Please, sir, we really need to get to Alabama," Jill said, trying to plead my case. "He'll be fine."

But it didn't work.

"I'm not going to get up in the air and have you have a panic attack. We'd have to turn the entire plane around and land. I'm sorry; you need to get off now."

Remember, this was in front of an entire plane full of people. People who had connecting flights to catch, plans to pursue, family to meet, and business meetings to make. I don't know if you've ever noticed, but people on flights are not the most patient humans on the earth, and the flight was getting more and more delayed the longer this conversation went on.

"I'm sorry," the pilot said, his tone now getting firm. "I'm not taking that chance. Get off now."

And so we did.

Completely embarrassed, Jill and I grabbed our carry-on bags from the overhead compartment and started down the Jetway.

"Hold on," the pilot said, calling us back. For a second, we thought he'd had a change of heart, but we were wrong. Instead, he decided it was too dangerous to let us get off the plane before they removed our luggage from the cargo hold underneath.

Apparently, he was suspicious that we were terrorists who'd planted something in our bags to blow up the plane. I guess he thought I was acting, playing it all up to get off the plane.

Or at least, that's where my mind was going . . . who knows.

Jill and I had to stand up in front of a plane full of frustrated passengers for thirty minutes while they found and removed our luggage underneath. They finally let us get off the plane, and some very nice ladies at the desk inside told us that they would let us try to fly again in six hours.

In other words, we got put in time-out.

So, if you are keeping score at home, I'd managed to add confusion and embarrassment to my anxiety and depression.

I was horrified. Humiliated. And anxious.

I felt terrible for everyone on the plane. I felt horrible for my wife. And I just kept apologizing to everyone.

## THE ROLLINS TO THE RESCUE

If you haven't figured this out yet, my wife is amazing. She sat there consoling me. What she knew (but didn't want to say) was that waiting six hours wouldn't change much. Unless she changed something, there was no guarantee I would be able to sit on the next plane.

If that was the case, we might never get to Alabama.

She got up and called our good friend Jimmy Rollins to ask him for some advice. Jimmy is a pastor and a friend. He is a sought-after speaker and always has a full schedule. But when she told him what was going on, he immediately told her he was on his way.

Yes, you read that right. And no, he was not in Dallas at the time.

He was at an airport somewhere else in the country. But whatever plans Jimmy had, they were going to have to wait; that's just the kind of friend he is. Next thing I knew, Jimmy was hugging me in the middle of the Dallas airport and asking if I was ready to go to Alabama with him by my side.

Then he walked up to the desk at our gate and said, "What do I need to pay to get the seat next to the Johnsons?"

It's tough to describe how far a friendship like that goes for those of us who struggle with mental health.

Six hours after I'd been kicked off the plane, I was reboarding a flight. This time, Jill and Jimmy were on either side of me, giving me pep talks and praying. Embarrassment and gratitude often go hand in hand. I can't tell you how thankful I was for their love and support, but somewhere deep down, I just kept thinking about how messed up I must have been if I couldn't even get on a plane without my friends.

After a few tears and lots of prayers, we made it to Alabama.

I survived.

And when we got off the plane and arrived at the hotel, someone else was waiting for us. Irene Rollins, Jimmy's wife, was standing there, smiling. Not only had Jimmy changed his entire schedule to fly with us to Alabama, but when he told his wife what he was doing, she dropped everything and caught the first flight to meet us there.

Our friends changed their entire schedules around and traveled a long distance just to have dinner with us that night and tell us that they loved us. They were there simply to tell us they believed in us and that they were going to fight for us.

Thank God for people like them. I don't have words for how much their friendship means to us.

# DAY ONE

The next day, Pastor Chris graciously set aside everything he was doing to spend several hours with Jill and me. If you know Pastor Chris or know anything about the schedule of a lead pastor, you know how irresponsible that is. But like Jimmy and Irene, he decided to drop everything and help.

He didn't *have* time for us; he *made* time for us.

We sat down in his office, and I let it rip. For several painful and tearful hours, I told him everything. I opened up about the anxiety, the depression, the hopelessness, the day on the side of the highway, and how difficult it was to get to Alabama.

Typically, when you open up like that to your pastor, you expect him to cry along with you or walk around the table, hug you, and tell you everything is going to be okay.

Nope.

Not my pastor.

And thank God because that's not what I needed that day. Pastor Chris looked me directly in the eyes and said, "Shawn, look at me. You're a fighter. It's time to start fighting." I opened my mouth to find some sort of rebuttal, but his stare made it clear that he wasn't done yet.

"It's time for you to stop being mad at yourself and start being mad at the Enemy. This anxiety is not about you. This depression is not about you; this hopelessness is not about you. There's a very real Enemy, and he wants to kill, steal, and destroy your life. It's time you got mad at him. It's time you blamed him. And it's time you started fighting."

When he finished, I didn't have any words. I didn't need any words. Something new was stirring in the depths of my soul.

I want you to know right now that no matter how long you've dealt with anxiety or depression or no matter how long your loved one has struggled with it, this does not have to be the way the story ends. But it is time to start fighting.

You are in the middle of a fight. And it's important to know who you're fighting. You're not fighting anxiety; you're not fighting depression; and you're not fighting hopelessness. You are fighting Satan. The devil. The Enemy.

Call him whatever you want, but he is very real, and he wants to steal from, kill, and destroy the very real plans that God has for your life. Remember, those aren't my words; they are Jesus' words: "The thief comes only to steal and kill and destroy; I have come that they may have life, and have it to the full" (John 10:10).

And the apostle Paul said it this way: "For our struggle is not against flesh and blood, but against the rulers, against the authorities, against the powers of this dark world and against the spiritual forces of evil in the heavenly realms" (Ephesians 6:12).

## FIGHTING WORDS

Satan doesn't create anything on his own. All he ever does is try to twist the things that God has made into something negative.

Think about fear. Remember earlier when I mentioned that facilitating anxiety (healthy fear) is actually from God? In its original state, fear isn't a bad thing. It's a healthy emotion that keeps us safe and on our toes, and at times, it helps us perform our best. The problem is, Satan loves to try to twist God's gifts to make them feel like curses.

Sadness is another example. When you lose something or someone you love, it's necessary to feel sad. That sadness is a sign that we actually care. That we actually love. But when the Enemy twists sadness into depression, it feels like the sadness switch is broken and doom is inevitable.

That's how Satan works. Every day he is on a horrible mission to twist God's gifts into something he hopes will destroy you. He wants God-given emotions to become deep, debilitating, unhealthy anxiety and depression that steal our ability to walk in God's calling on our lives.

This is not a shock to God and should not be a shock to us. Two thousand years ago, Jesus told us this would happen, and he also told us not to worry because he would take care of things. He said it like this: "In this world you will have trouble. But take heart! I have overcome the world" (John 16:33).

We are broken people living in a broken world, and every now and then, we might have to fight to experience the very freedom that Christ has already provided us with.

But the good news is *we can* fight back.

We can be victorious. We can overcome. We can conquer things like anxiety and depression. We can experience freedom on levels that we may have never thought possible.

Why?

Because greater is he who is within me than he that is in the world (1 John 4:4). The power and the presence of Jesus Christ working in and through our lives is greater than anything Satan can do. He may want to use anxiety and depression to steal from, kill, or destroy us, but when we stand up and fight—when we decide to attack back—he always *loses*. He can't take our peace. He can't steal our joy. He can't destroy our purpose.

Those things are rightfully ours.

We just have to be willing to fight for them.

Remember the verse we started this journey with. "It is for freedom that Christ has set us free. Stand firm, then, and do not let yourselves be burdened again by a yoke of slavery" (Galatians 5:1).

Freedom is a gift.

It is our God-given right that has been purchased for us.

But in order to enjoy it and experience it, we have to take a stand. We have to work for it. Sometimes that freedom will come easily and naturally, but other times, we will need to fight.

While I sat across the table from Pastor Chris, something clicked for me. I felt like I was on my last leg, but something changed when he called me a fighter.

"I can see it in your eyes," he said. "You are a fighter. It's time to fight."

And now I want to say the same thing to you. Whether you're fighting for yourself or you're fighting for a loved one, it's time to fight.

With tears still streaming down my face, I admitted I didn't even know where to start. As those words came out of my mouth, they were accompanied by so much shame and disappointment in myself. I'd been the lead pastor of a church for fifteen years; how was it possible that I didn't even know where to start this holy battle? How could I have let myself hit a rock bottom like this? My job is to help other people get out of the pit, not sit at the bottom of it with tears in my eyes.

Or at least, that's what I thought.

"Here's what you are going to do," he said without skipping a beat. "You're going to start praying. You're going to start worshiping. You're going to start fighting!"

And trust me, if you are thinking, *That's it?* you are keying into exactly how I was feeling.

*Pray about what?*

*Worship? Huh?*

I didn't know how right he was. I was walking into an all-out war, a dogfight for my freedom. And prayer and worship proved to be some of the very weapons I needed to relearn how to use.

If something is stirring deep in your soul right now, it's because you are realizing (whether for the first time or the hundredth time) that you have the power to attack back.

That day, Jill and I knew it was time to start fighting, so we went to the war room and took prayer and worship with us. And now, I want to teach you how to do the same exact thing.

# USING WORSHIP
# AS A WEAPON

"The rules are simple," Pastor Chris told my wife and me. "Take this Bluetooth speaker into that room, blast some worship music, and start worshiping and praying out loud together."

Jill *loved* those instructions. I *hated* them.

I'm a pastor, so you wouldn't think that would be a difficult task for me, but I can't stand praying with my wife. She's an incredible prayer warrior, and I feel like a stuttering idiot. Even after all these years of marriage, this far into my relationship with God, it still feels awkward for me to pray with her at length.

I hope that is freeing for some of you. Stop feeling guilty. It's not just you!

"That's right," he continued, "it's time to start worshiping. You're both going to pray out loud for thirty straight minutes at the volume of the music."

When Pastor Chris saw the deer-in-the-headlights look I gave him, he explained the method to his madness. He reminded us we were in a battle, and the first two weapons we needed to use were prayer and worship.

The whole thing was a little confusing. Prayer doesn't fix my anxiety; at times it gives me even more of it. And worship is something we do in church services that, truthfully, makes me feel insecure and often makes my feet hurt when they have us standing for so long.

I thought, *I'm here fighting for my life. We are going to war. And our weapons of choice are prayer and worship?*

But then he said something that changed the trajectory of my life: "Satan hates it when we pray like this. It destroys him."

That's what I needed to hear. His words instantly brought me back to something that had happened less than a year prior, an experience that changed my family's lives forever. An event where I felt like God was telling me to stop seeing worship as singing songs in church and begin viewing it as a weapon to battle for my freedom.

## THE WALLS OF JERICHO

I had been studying and preaching in the book of Joshua, the man who miraculously took the nation of Israel across the Jordan River into the promised land. But when he got into the promised land, as I mentioned earlier, he still had to fight thirty-one battles to take possession of it.

The very first battle is somewhat famous. Even if you haven't been in church much, you may have heard of the Battle of Jericho. It's this crazy story where God instructed the nation of Israel to march around Jericho for seven straight days. And on the last day, God told them to start worshiping, singing, yelling, praising God, and playing instruments.

The interesting thing is, the trumpets God instructed them to play were sometimes used as a battle cry before the battle but were most often used to celebrate after a victory. The Israelites would always fire up the worship music after they won a battle. But in this case, God told them to start worshiping, singing, yelling, and playing those instruments *before* they saw the victory.

What?

Celebrate before they had anything to celebrate? Worship before they saw the outcome they wanted? That doesn't make any sense, and yet that's exactly what God called them to do.

And the results were mind-blowing. You can read all about it in Joshua 6. Essentially, as soon as they started worshiping, Jericho's walls, which were securely barred, miraculously fell, and the Israelites were able to overcome the city.

The Israelites didn't have a chance on their own strength. However, right in the middle of their confusion, fear, anxiety, depression, and (I have to believe) feelings of hopelessness, God showed up in a spectacular way. They experienced freedom and a victory they never dreamed possible. And the whole thing was put in motion with a weapon called worship.

Sometimes we worship because we've had a victory. But sometimes we worship *until we see one.*

God demonstrated to Joshua that there would be times in life where worship would be the way to victory. Worship will be the way you defeat your Enemy. Worship will be what brings you the very freedom you so badly desire.

All of that sounds great in theory. The story of Joshua and the role of worship was a lot of fun to preach about, but then one night, right in the middle of the series, this concept became real for me.

# THE ICU

It was a Friday night, and Jill and I were doing what we usually do on Friday nights these days—taking our boys to practices and games (obviously). I was at Ashton's football practice when Jill called me.

"Ethan doesn't look good," she said. "He looks kind of pale. I'm a little worried. Maybe I should take him to the hospital."

Ethan had just been on a mission trip in Africa with our church, and it had Jill worried that he might have brought back a bug from the journey. To be honest, that sounded like an overreaction to me, but I wasn't about to be the dad who talks his spouse out of a hospital visit. The last time I'd done that, Ashton actually had a broken foot, and I'd told him to "man up" for a week before finally taking him in. So I was determined not to be that guy again.

"Yeah, sure," I said as a caring parent would. "Run him up there."

A few hours later, I got another call from Jill. She told me they were about to check out and head home. Ethan saw a nurse and then the doctor, and they didn't notice anything out of the ordinary.

Then all of a sudden, she got real quiet.

"Wait. What?" Something shifted in her voice. She was no longer talking to me; she was talking to somebody else in the room. "Excuse me. What's happening? Ethan? Are you okay? I don't understand."

My stomach sank. "Babe, what's going on?"

"I don't know," she said, now frantically crying into the phone. "Shawn, I don't know what's going on. I think you should come here."

"Jill, what's happening?" I asked again in desperation, feeling helpless from the other side of the phone.

"I don't know. Everybody's running around and yelling. They just said something about the ICU." Then she paused again. "Shawn, Ethan is unconscious. Start praying right now and get here fast."

My son went into something called septic shock. They rushed him to the ICU, where we would spend the next five nights. I felt like I was in an episode of a medical mystery drama. The infectious disease unit would come into our room several times a day and ask every question you could imagine.

Where in Africa was he?

What did he eat?

What did he drink?

Who did he see?

Where did he go?

We were at the best hospital in a multistate area, but no one could figure out what was killing my son. He was hooked up to twenty different IV bags, and the care professionals were trying to give him medicine for a disease they could not diagnose. After being in the ICU all week, he had experienced respiratory failures and septic shock, and several of his organs were starting to shut down. By day five, they still couldn't figure out what was wrong with him, and the doctor began to have conversations with me that sounded like this: "Here is the percentage of chance that he will live. Here is the percentage of chance that he won't."

It was the longest five days of our lives.

On night five, at about three o'clock in the morning, I got up and started walking around the hospital. I couldn't control my sobbing any longer. I started talking to God.

For the ten thousandth time in the last five days I said, "Would you please heal my son." I remember just repeating that phrase, "God heal my son. God heal my son. God, please heal my son."

Some were whispers.

Some were screams.

Remember, I'd been teaching our church about the story of Joshua for several weeks. The theme of the entire teaching series was that we don't have to live afraid because we can stand on the promises of God's Word. And the key verse of the whole series was Joshua 1:9: "Be strong and courageous. Do not be afraid; do not be discouraged, for the LORD your God will be with you wherever you go."

How ironic.

For several weeks, I'd been teaching thousands of people how to not be afraid, and that night I was more fearful than I've been in my entire life. Through tears, I kept asking, "God, what do I do? I don't think I can reconcile this in my brain. If my son dies because he went on a mission trip to tell people about Jesus, if that is our story, if that is how it ends, I don't think I can make sense of that in my mind. I don't know if I can go on. How am I going to continue to believe in you? How am I going to continue to preach about you? How am I going to reconcile this in my brain? God, help me. I've never been more afraid, and I don't know what to do."

Suddenly, through all the confusion, I realized the real question I was trying to ask. "What do I do when I'm standing on your promises that say I don't have to be afraid, but I still feel afraid?"

I'll never forget the response. I didn't hear God's audible voice. But a thought I never would've come up with on my own hit me so clearly that it must have been God. *When you're standing on my Word that says you don't have to be afraid, but you still feel afraid, put your foot down, and put your hands up.*

I knew exactly what God was saying to me. This is what I'd been trying to articulate to our church for several weeks. God gives us promises in Scripture; our job is to put our foot down and stand on those promises while we lift our hands and worship. Claim the promises and then praise as if they've already come true.

Sometimes you will worship because of a victory, but other times you worship until you see one. So, put your foot down, and put your hands up because it's time to use worship as a weapon!

God was telling me to do the very same thing he had told Joshua to do. And I believe that's exactly what God wants you to do right now. I know that what you're up against feels impossible. I know that what you're up against scares you to death. I know the walls in front of you feel like a prison that will never come down, so I'm telling you, starting right now, I want you to *worship till the walls fall down.*

That night, walking around the hospital by myself, was the scariest moment of my life. It was panic, fear, and uncertainty all at the same time, but I put my hands up in the air, I stomped my foot on the floor, and I just began to stand on the promises of God:

- No matter what comes my way, I don't have to be afraid because even if I can't feel it, I know God is with me (Joshua 1:9).
- God has a plan for my life and for my loved ones, even if I don't understand it (Jeremiah 29:11).

- God is working in my life and in my son's life right now, even if I can't see it (Romans 8:28).
- No weapon formed against me shall prosper (Isaiah 54:17).
- Greater is he who is within me than he that is in the world (1 John 4:4).
- In all things, I am more than a conqueror through him who loves me (Romans 8:37).

I started stating these promises out loud, telling Satan what God has to say about my future. Before I knew it, I was using worship as a weapon to battle for my sanity, peace, and freedom. If you happened to be walking around the hospital that night, here's what you would've heard:

> *God, I know your Word promises that you're with me and that you'll never leave me or forsake me. I know I don't have to be afraid. I know you have a plan, even when I can't see it or understand it. Your Word says no weapon formed against me shall prosper. God, I pray for my son Ethan. Greater are you inside of my son than any disease or virus his body is fighting. Ethan is more than a conqueror. God, I worship you tonight. I know that you're good, even though I'm hurting. I know that you're good, even though I'm confused. I know that you're good, even though my son is sick. I know that you're with us, and I know you are still a miracle-working God who is in the miracle-working business. I stand on your Word, and I put my hands in the air, and I praise you tonight.*

I circled the hospital standing on God's Word with my hands in the air, crying buckets of tears.

Slowly but surely, I began to pull it together.

Slowly but surely, I began to feel the peace of God.

Slowly but surely, my confidence started coming back.

I'll save this entire story for another time, but just to let you off the emotional hook, some unbelievable things happened. My son was miraculously healed. Doctors in the hospital were literally using the word *miracle*. A few days later, we were able to leave the hospital, and today, he is 100 percent healthy and whole. My family and I learned firsthand that worship is an absolute weapon. It is a weapon of mass destruction that destroys Satan's ability to mess with your mind, your will, and your emotions.

# THE WAR ROOM

I guess I shouldn't have been surprised that these were Pastor Chris's instructions. Jill and I hit the war room, armed with the weapon of worship, ready to battle for my freedom from anxiety and depression.

Afterward, I found some songs that talk about peace, freedom, and victory, and I continued to wield the weapon of worship by putting those songs on repeat. Around that time, our worship team at Red Rocks Church released a song called "Breakthrough," and I started every single day with it. Sometimes all I could do was listen to the words of the song. Other times, I had the strength to whisper the lyrics. Then sometimes, I had the strength to sing them out loud.

I declared God's promises over my life every day. *I will see a victory. No weapon formed against me will prosper. There will be a day when I will have a breakthrough. This will be my testimony, not my long-standing reality, in Jesus' name.*

Worship sustained me through one of the most challenging seasons of my life. I leaned on it every day. I worshiped in the mornings, in the car, and every night. Whenever I started to feel an anxiety attack come on, I played worship music. I don't know where I would be without this weapon called worship.

My challenge to you, even if worship music is not your genre of choice, is to ask around, get online, do what you need to do to find some songs that speak to your soul. Find songs that declare the goodness of God and talk about finding peace, joy, purpose, and freedom. Create a playlist and go to battle with it daily.

## WHY WORSHIP?

At this point, you might be asking how worshiping could possibly change your situation. Great question.

In Scripture God taught us two unique ways to experience his presence. The first is the public gathering. There are several reasons we gather together as a church, but one of them is because God promised, "Where two or three gather in my name, there am I with them" (Matthew 18:20). The other way is worship. Psalm 22:3 tells us that God inhabits the praise of his people. Which is a fancy way of saying, when we worship, God's presence shows up! And that is a big deal because here are the byproducts of spending time in God's presence:

1. Peace (Philippians 4:6–7)
2. Joy (Psalm 16:11)

3. Rest (Exodus 33:14)
4. Confidence (Jeremiah 17:7)
5. Guidance (Exodus 15:13)
6. Protection (Psalm 5:11; Isaiah 41:10)
7. Power (Joshua 1:9; Ephesians 3:20)

What do peace, joy, rest, confidence, guidance, protection, and power all have in common? They are the opposite of fear, worry, anxiety, and depression. In other words, God is the solution! If we just spend time in God's presence, he promises to give us the very things we are praying for every day.

If you have anxiety or depression, I want you to continue praying for peace, joy, rest, confidence, guidance, protection, and power. But I also want you to realize that worship will bring those things into your life.

Worship *defeats* depression.

Worship *overcomes* anxiety.

Worship *restores* confidence.

Worship is a weapon that can defeat the things the Enemy is trying to use to take you out.

I get the privilege of passing on the same challenge my pastor gave me. It's time you started fighting. It's time to attack anxiety! Stop being so mad at yourself. Stop being so hard on yourself. Stop blaming yourself and start blaming the Enemy. It's time to get angry and go to war. It's time to begin battling for the freedom Jesus has given you, and one of the best ways to fight for your peace, joy, purpose, and freedom is to use this weapon called worship.

# PRAYING LIKE A WARRIOR

A few months ago, I was doing an interview about dealing with anxiety and depression, and the interviewer asked, "What would you tell someone who is feeling absolutely overwhelmed with anxiety right now? Imagine they have no idea where to start; what would you say?"

"Put on some worship music," I said without hesitation. "Start praising and start praying. And as you do, talk to God real raw and honest."

Don't hold back.

Don't hold any punches.

Don't talk formally.

Don't try to make a speech.

Talk to your Father and tell him exactly what you want and exactly how you feel. Tell him exactly what you need. Ask him for help. Ask him for strength. Ask him for courage. And most of all, ask him for peace. Then get real intentional about telling God the specific things in your life for which you are thankful.

I'm telling you, this combination of worship and prayer is deadly to anxiety and depression.

But if you are anything like me, when you hear that word *prayer*, just about every insecurity begins rising to the surface.

Heading into the war room to worship was one thing, but to be honest, the whole prayer piece was the part that made me nervous. Remember the rules; we had to pray out loud for thirty minutes. For my wife, the prayer warrior, that was a walk in the park. But honestly, I'm more of a short, sweet, and to-the-point kind of guy when it comes to prayer.

I knew I was in a battle for my life, and Pastor Chris assured me that prayer was the spiritual weapon I had to learn to love. I knew it was going to be more challenging for me than it was for Jill, but I was desperate for change and was ready to take my prayer life to a new level. Although, if I'm totally honest, I had plenty of self-doubts.

Maybe you can relate to that. Have you ever looked around at other Christians and wondered how they are so spiritual? How can they pray for so long? Like me, have you ever doubted that you are a prayer warrior?

If that's you, you aren't alone.

If you've ever been intimidated by prayer, this chapter is for you. If you've ever called other people prayer warriors but never believed that about yourself, this chapter is for you. Because I was wrong to think that I couldn't battle with this weapon called prayer, and you are wrong to think that about yourself too.

And that takes us to a story about a man named Gideon.

# MIGHTY WARRIOR

There is an epic story tucked away in Judges 6. At that point, the nation of Israel was under oppression. The Midianites had taken over, and God's people were scared for their lives.

One day, an Israelite named Gideon was hiding in a winepress when an angel of the Lord appeared. Check out the angel's opening line: "The LORD is with you, mighty warrior" (Judges 6:12). That's quite a statement to make to a man who is hiding in a winepress, fearing for his life. But the angel didn't stop there. He doubled down on his statement and told Gideon he would be the one to save the Israelites from the Midianites.

Gideon didn't buy any of it.

And you can't blame him.

Overwhelmed with fear, worry, and anxiety, he started making every excuse in the book. As if the angel didn't already know, he explained how his family was the weakest in town. Then he went on to talk about how even among his family, he was the worst candidate.

Don't you love how honest the Bible is?

This is a guy I can relate to. He was scared to death and didn't have a clue what to do. But the angel reminded him of the most important piece of the puzzle. God was going with him. Which meant Gideon could do this; he would experience a victory because he was a mighty warrior.

Before we go any further, you need to hear the same thing. Prayer is an intimidating topic, but the good news is, your Creator is in this with you. He isn't sitting off to the side with a timesheet, shaking his head at your inability to pray a long prayer with charisma. He is in this process with you.

And that means you are a mighty prayer warrior.

Even if prayer has never been your thing, that's all about to change because God is going with you. It's time to start praying like a warrior.

Listen, you may not feel like a mighty warrior, but you are one. And it has very little to do with you and everything to do with the fact that God is going with you.

The Bible is full of men and women who felt incredibly unqualified to step up to the task. And every time, God reminded them that he was going with them.

Even before you say your first word or take one step onto the battlefield, I'm telling you: you are a mighty warrior. And beginning to battle for you or your loved one's freedom from anxiety and depression is going to be a life-changing event.

## WHERE DO I START?

You may be thinking, *Great pep talk, Shawn, but when it comes to prayer, I don't even know where to begin.*

Well fortunately, the Bible's got our backs once again.

Prayer was a pivotal part of Paul's life, and in his letter to the church in Philippi, he gave us an easy formula to attack anxiety and learn to live free.

Before we get there, I want to remind you (once again) that Paul didn't always have it all together. We think of Paul as the all-star Christian, and he was, but he also once wrote, "We do not want you to be uninformed, brothers and sisters, about the troubles we experienced in the province of Asia. We were under great pressure, far beyond our ability to endure, so that we *despaired of life itself*" (2 Corinthians 1:8, emphasis added).

Why am I sharing that verse again?

Because I find it so comforting.

Paul was a sold-out, all-in, church-planting, kingdom-of-God-building machine. He was a pastor, leader, and person of great faith. And yet, he dealt with fear, worry, anxiety, depression, and hopelessness on such an intense level that there were times that he "despaired of life itself." On paper, he was doing everything right, and yet he still felt like everything was wrong.

Let that free you up today.

If you are anything like me, you know the guilt, shame, and embarrassment that comes with following Jesus but still struggling with anxiety and depression. We think we must be doing something wrong if we are still struggling.

The thing is, if the apostle Paul, a man who wrote nearly half of the New Testament, dealt with this stuff, maybe it's time we realize it's okay for us to struggle too. You aren't a superhuman; you are a human being just like the rest of us.

Okay. Back to prayer.

God knows we're broken people living in a broken world. And he knows the reality of anxiety and depression and the real effects they have on every area of our lives. So he got real specific in his Word:

Do not be anxious about anything, but in every situation, by prayer and petition, with thanksgiving, present your requests to God. And the peace of God, which transcends all understanding, will guard your hearts and your minds in Christ Jesus. (Philippians 4:6–7)

I love that passage.

According to Paul, when anxiety attacks, you can attack back. You don't have to be anxious about anything because you can talk to God about everything.

It's time to fight. And our weapon is prayer. It's time to take it out of its holster and put it to work!

Do you want to *attack* anxiety?

Do you want to *defeat* depression?

Paul gave us our battle plan: *petitions* and *thanksgiving*.

This is a deadly combo, which is why Paul saved it for dealing with anxious thoughts. He knew how brutal that anxiety monster could be, so he took time in his short letter to Philippi to address it directly.

When anxiety comes at you, attack back with petition and thanksgiving.

## Petition

Put simply, prayer is communicating with God.

It's an umbrella term. There are many aspects to it, and there are all sorts of different strategies for approaching it. But at the end of the day, the concept is incredibly simple. Prayer is just talking to God, telling him what's on your mind and heart, and telling him your thoughts, cares, joys, concerns, worries, fears, hopes, and dreams.

According to Paul, one of the secrets to overcoming anxiety is to "make your requests known to God" (Philippians 4:6 MEV). God invites us to get in the habit of telling him all about the things that are bothering us.

You parents understand this, don't you?

When one of your kids is struggling, the last thing you want them to do is keep it to themselves. You love it when they come to you and talk it out.

God gives us the same invitation. He is our loving Father who wants to sit and listen to all our petitions.

That's where Jill and I started that day in the war room. We spent some time talking to God. We got real, raw, and honest with him, telling him exactly how we felt and exactly what we wanted from him. Over the weeks, those petitions became less about all the things we wanted and started to become more about peace. A peace that surpasses understanding.

A peace that may not even make sense.

Did you know that peace is possible right now?

Considering the storm you're in the middle of, you may have just laughed out loud at the thought of being at peace, but it's true. Considering your level of anxiety, considering your level of depression, considering your level of hopelessness, you may feel like peace is impossible. But remember what we talked about a few chapters ago: God's in the business of making the impossible possible.

God says he will bring us a peace that doesn't even make sense in this situation. A peace that passes all our understanding. All we have to do is ask!

## Thanksgiving

The second half of the equation Paul gave us involves gratitude. He instructed us to present our petitions with *thanksgiving*.

If you were to ask most of us if we are grateful for what God has done, we would say, "Yes, of course I'm grateful." But most of us also don't say thank you to God very often out loud.

There's something powerful about telling God what you think out loud. Your next prayer session could simply be you making a list of things you are thankful for and then telling God all about how much you appreciate the things on your list and the life he has given you. I'm serious. Try it. You'll be amazed at how much better you feel afterward.

Years ago, I was going through a time of real depression, and I was sitting with a friend of mine, complaining about it.

"Are you praying about it?" he asked.

"Are you kidding me?" I responded, a bit annoyed by the question. "That's all I pray about every day."

But he wasn't finished. "When you are praying, what are you saying? Is it just a list of complaints? Is it just all the things you want? All the things you need? All the explanations of how bad things are?"

That caught me off guard. I had to think about it for a second.

"Yep, that's pretty much it," I told him. "I tell God all my problems, then I complain for a bit about how bad things are and say *amen*."

"What if you tried talking to God about how thankful you are?"

I only was using half of the weapon. I was great at the petition part, as you probably are too. Anyone with kids knows how naturally asking for things comes to us. We've been asking our parents for things since we were able to speak.

Asking comes easy. It's the saying thank you part that takes some intentionality.

My friend went on to encourage me to start telling God all the things I'm thankful for, and then he said one of the most profound things I've ever heard: "It's hard to be depressed and thankful at the same time."

That line has been a game changer for me.

When I'm feeling down, gratitude changes things. By making a list of all the things I am thankful for, my perspective shifts.

I have found that simply making that list and then telling God all about the things on it changes my mindset.

I try to start each day with a few minutes of gratitude. Before I do anything else, I begin by thanking God for all the blessings I have, and it changes the course of my entire day.

And here's the good news. When you do this enough, eventually, it just starts becoming a habit. When I start putting a streak together of a few days, I begin waking up in the morning and thinking, *Do you know what? Today I'm just deciding that I'm going to have a good day. I'm going to start my day by focusing on the things I have to be thankful for. I'm going to say them out loud and watch how much peace and joy come into my heart long before anything else has a chance to get in there.*

And if you want to take gratitude to a whole new level, call somebody up and share some good news with them. Just say, "I just wanted to tell you that I have some things to be thankful for. I wanted to tell you how good God has been to me." They'll probably think it's a bit strange at first, but gratitude is contagious. Before long, they'll be passing along the things they are grateful for to someone else.

This is the power of prayer. Don't overcomplicate it, especially in the heat of the moment. Few things attack anxiety and defeat depression faster than gratitude. Tell God everything you need (petition), then start bragging about all the things he has already done for you (thanksgiving); you'll be amazed at how far that takes you.

# YOU CAN DO THIS

Every day for the next two weeks, Jill and I went to the war room to battle for thirty minutes at a time.

Was it easy every day? No.

Did we feel like doing it every day? No.

Did I feel immediate miraculous results every single time we did it? No.

But after two weeks in the war room, taking ground a half hour at a time, I can tell you with all honesty that I left Alabama feeling better, healthier, and stronger than when I arrived. I left with newfound hope for the future and a newfound peace in my heart. I knew I had a lot of work to do still, but I also knew I wasn't the same man who broke down on the side of the road. I was beginning to experience a new level of peace.

My prayer for you is that you would do the same thing. Take these last two chapters to heart and start attacking anxiety and defeating depression.

It's not difficult; it just takes effort.

And you can do this!

Number one, put on some worship music and just start praising God. Number two, talk to him in a real, raw, and honest way. Tell God exactly what you need. Ask, beg, scream, and yell if you have to. And if the words are escaping you, just whisper, "Help!"

And then start saying thank you.

At first, it will feel like trying to push a semitruck up a giant hill. But it will get easier and more comfortable as you go. And it will start to feel more and more natural along the way. This is just like working out. At first, it's difficult and uncomfortable, but the more you start to feel the effects of it, the more you'll begin to look forward to it. Tell God what you're thankful for, tell him out loud, tell him often, and tell somebody else.

Be real.

Be raw.

Be honest.

Ask God for exactly what you want and need.

And then say thank you!

Say it often.

Say it out loud.

And the result, we're promised, is the peace we've been craving all along. Use that weapon called worship side by side with prayer and watch what God does with it. This kind of prayer is a prescription for peace!

You may be feeling like Gideon right now, thinking there's no way God's calling you to be a prayer warrior. But as you head into this, I want you to know: you are a *mighty warrior*. Take this to heart; I mean it. Even if you don't feel like it, the God of the universe is going with you. That means you are a mighty warrior!

You can do this.

You are going to attack anxiety and defeat depression and experience levels of freedom that you have never felt before. As you step into battle and start to use this weapon of prayer, remember God is with you.

You're perfect in his sight.

He loves you.

He's working in your life even when you can't see it. He has a plan even when you can't feel it, and he's with you every step of the way.

You are a *prayer warrior*!

# REMEMBERING TO ATTACK BACK

Have you ever been sick and tired of being sick and tired? It took me a while to get to that point, but I finally got there the day I broke down on the side of the road.

I was sick of the panic attacks.

I was sick of the anxiety.

I was sick of the depression.

And most of all, I was sick and tired of letting those things control my life. It was time to do something about it.

I bet you (or your loved one) know that feeling. And this may sound illogical to you at first, but that's really good news. Sometimes you have to get to the point of desperation before you are ready to put your foot down and say enough is enough.

When you realize you aren't destined to stay stuck playing the victim card for the rest of your life, you are ready to get proactive and *fight*.

You are ready to start standing on the truth and attacking back!

Remember, when we talk about attacking anxiety, we are talking about attacking the one causing our anxiety. The one who wants to steal, kill, and destroy our lives. Get ready for a dogfight. After all, we are fighting against the devil, and the devil doesn't play fair. He'll wield anxiety, depression, hopelessness, and any other terrible weapons he has in his arsenal to fight dirty.

And so, to get ready to attack back, the next question to ask is: Where is this battle taking place?

# THE BATTLEGROUND

If I've learned anything about mental health over the years, it's that much of the battle begins in the mind. Call it Satan or just my own propensity to get down on myself, but the way I'm feeling is typically an overflow of my own thoughts. We are in a fight for our lives, and the entire battleground exists between our ears.

It's time to learn how to *take every thought captive* (2 Corinthians 10:5).

The Bible reminds us that we get to choose what we focus on. Have you ever thought about the fact that we can think about what we think about? We get to decide which thoughts we dwell on. It's our choice. And it's incredible how quickly our mood, confidence, and outlook on life change when we start focusing on the right things.

In the last chapter, we learned a prayer from Paul to help us avoid anxiety. I figured that was a big enough endeavor for one chapter, so what I didn't show you is that in the very next verse, he gave us the solution to winning the battle in our minds.

> Finally, brothers and sisters, whatever is true, whatever is noble, whatever is right, whatever is pure, whatever is lovely, whatever is admirable—if anything is excellent or praiseworthy—think about such things. (Philippians 4:8)

Did you catch that? Since Paul knew we would be fighting a battle and knew the battleground is the mind, he urged us to start thinking about what we think about.

Peace is *possible*.

The key to obtaining it is to start remembering all the amazing things God has already done in our lives. God has done so much for all of us over the years, but in the heat of battle, when we are in the middle of a storm, it can be easy to forget about all the good and focus on the bad. Which is why Paul urged us to start reflecting on the past and purposefully remember all the true, noble, right, pure, lovely, admirable, excellent, and praiseworthy things God has already done.

Remembering what God has done for us is a massive weapon for defeating anxiety and depression. This is similar to the thankfulness part of prayer we talked about in the last chapter, but in this chapter, we'll take it to a whole new level. Anxiety will attack, but tuning in to memories of God's victories in your life is how you attack back.

This theme is all throughout the Bible. One of my favorite stories about remembering what God has done is in Joshua 4. In chapter 6, we talked about that first battle Joshua and the Israelites faced when they got into the promised land, but before that moment, there was another amazing story of how God made a way for them to even get to the land. If you want the play-by-play, I'd encourage you to read the whole story (Joshua 1–6). In the meantime, here's the ESPN highlight version of the story.

## GO BACK TO GO FORWARD

When Moses died, his protégé, Joshua, took over leading the Israelites. Joshua's first week on the job was a bit hectic, to say the least. His task was to finally bring the people into the promised land after forty years of wandering in the wilderness. If you've read the story, you know the obstacle standing in their way was the Jordan River during flood season. Getting an entire nation through that river was an impossible task.

*Unless God intervened.*

Through a series of events we'll talk more about in part 4, God stopped the flow of the river, and for the second time in the Israelites' journey out of Egypt, the entire nation walked through on dry ground.

Picture that moment.

They had been dreaming of entering into the land for as long as they could remember, and God made a way. But just as they were about to sprint in and begin celebrating, God pumped the brakes. "Send twelve men back into the river," he told Joshua. "Tell them to bring back twelve large stones" (Joshua 4:1–3, paraphrased).

"I'm sorry?" Joshua said (at least that is how I picture it going in my head). "You just miraculously brought us through this thing, and now you want us to go back?"

*Yep.*

God knew just how quickly humans tend to forget things. So before running off into the promised land, he instructed Joshua to stop and set up a system to help them stand on the truth by remembering his faithfulness.

Check out the pep talk Joshua gave to the leaders he was sending back to the middle of the river.

> Go over before the ark of the LORD your God into the middle of the Jordan. Each of you is to take up a stone on his shoulder, according to the number of the tribes of the Israelites, to serve as a sign among you. In the future, when your children ask you, "What do these stones mean?" tell them that the flow of the Jordan was cut off before the ark of the covenant of the LORD. When it crossed the Jordan, the waters of the Jordan were cut off. These stones are to be a memorial to the people of Israel forever. (Joshua 4:5–7)

God knew they needed a memorial. Something to jog their memory when they went through seasons of doubt, fear, worry, anxiety, or depression in the future. While an entire nation watched (waiting even longer to enter the land), the men got the stones and built a memorial on the beach. They set up a system to remind themselves of God's faithfulness when they were feeling down. They made a memorial of the moment they thought their story was over—when their mission seemed impossible.

And it's a good thing they did because God knew something they did not: their journey was far from over.

As we talked about in chapters 1 and 6, once they got into the promised land, they were still going to have to fight. Even though they made it to the land, they still had thirty-one battles waiting for them.

Think about how much anxiety that would have caused them every day.

God knew what he was doing all along. He knew that every time anxiety reared its ugly head and they felt an anxiety attack coming on, they needed a memorial to remind them what they'd already been through.

God was giving them a weapon to *attack back*.

The power to access peace is often found in your ability to remember.

Remembering what God has done for you in the past will build your faith and bring you peace in the present. It's time that we do the same thing. It's time for us to *start remembering* what God's already brought us through. Before we go any further, we first need to go back and build a memorial. For the rest of this chapter, you will need a pen and some paper because our memorial will consist of three lists.

### List #1: Remember What God Has Brought You Through

For the first list, we are going to write out all the victories we've seen God help us win in our lives. I'm serious. If you are already rolling your eyes, just trust me for a minute. This is not some cheesy exercise that doesn't correlate with reality; this will change your life.

At least, it did for me.

Recently, a fantastic couple offered to take us (and one other couple) on an all-expenses-paid, four-day vacation—just the six of us. Jill and I felt so honored and so excited to go, so we packed our bags and jumped on a plane.

The first day was incredible, but as we were heading to bed, they informed us that the plan for day two was for the six of us to go on an all-day boat trip. My heart sank. For most people, a day on the water is a dream come true.

Not for me.

That plan sounded like an invitation to the outskirts of hell. Because of my anxiety and claustrophobia, anytime I find myself in a situation that I can't get out of, I start to feel anxious. I live in Colorado; I would love to ski more, but to ski, you have to get on the ski lift, which freaks me out because it is out of my control and I can't just jump off halfway up the mountain. I don't even like being in the back seat of a car when somebody else is driving on the highway because I can't control pulling over to the side of the road.

Boats make me anxious.

You may be thinking, *How in the world could you feel claustrophobic on a boat? You could not be more out in the open and free when you are on the water.* Well, to you, I would say: No. In the middle of the ocean where you can't see the shore, your boat is your only chance at survival. You are stuck.

It's interesting how anxiety hits us all slightly differently.

And to make matters worse, one of the couples on this trip were heroes to Jill and me. I'm serious. About a month before this trip, we were having dinner with some friends, and we were playing the "You get to have a meal with one person on the entire planet, who are you choosing?" game.

I picked this guy. He is someone I've always looked up to.

Which is incredible news when that is the guy you get invited to spend an entire weekend with. But terrible news when that is the guy you have to tell you aren't currently stable enough to get on a boat.

But I couldn't do it. I was so convinced I would have an anxiety attack in the middle of the ocean and completely humiliate myself in front of this guy I've admired for years. Are you starting to see why this day felt like the outskirts of hell to me?

That night, Jill and I were getting ready for bed, and I lost it. "Babe, I can't get on that boat," I said. "I'm already having anxiety about it, and we aren't even there yet. What am I going to do?"

Now, if you don't deal with anxiety, this may be hard for you to relate to. But those of you who are in this with me know we can begin to have anxiety just thinking about a future event that could possibly cause us anxiety.

And yes, that means we have *anxiety* about our *anxiety*.

At that point, I was pacing back and forth in our room, in this beautiful house, on this all-expenses-paid-for vacation, and all I could think about was the inevitable panic attack coming my way in the morning.

"Okay, honey," Jill said without skipping a beat. She loves the water, but as you've probably picked up by now, she's also amazing and is always in my corner. "In the morning, I'll just explain to them that we are going to stay here at the house. We'll wish them well, and you and I can stay here by ourselves. Everything will be fine."

"You better not be fooling," I said, summoning my inner Lloyd Christmas from *Dumb and Dumber*. Feeling embarrassed but also incredibly grateful for my wife's patience, I turned off the light and went to bed.

But I couldn't sleep.

My mind was racing. Partly because of my anxiety, partly because I felt stupid, and partly because I was trying to figure out how in the world I was going to tell these amazing people that we didn't want to go on an all-day boat trip with them. Anxiety was pending, and I couldn't sleep.

As I lay in bed, staring at the ceiling, I started to think about a sermon I'd preached a while back. I told the church that whenever you are struggling, one of the best things you can do is start reminding yourself of all the things God has already brought you through. "Let your memories preach to you about God's faithfulness," I'd encouraged. "You've been here before. God came through back then, and he's going to do it again."

"Well," I whispered audibly, "I should probably start smoking what I'm selling." (Forgive the analogy; I live in Colorado.)

I got up, took out my phone, opened the Notes app, and started making a list of all the things God had already brought me through:

1. My biological father left town the day he realized he had gotten my mom, a high school girl, pregnant. I've never seen him. I've never met him. I've never heard from him. It's been difficult, but God got me through.

2. My mom developed a heroin addiction, and when I was an infant, she put me in a car seat and left me on a stranger's porch with a note to call a certain phone number. And then she went and jumped off a bridge onto a highway into oncoming traffic to kill herself. Somehow, she survived the jump, just crushing her legs and breaking a bunch of bones. I grew up telling everyone who'd listen that my mom was my hero, and she was! But because of some life choices she made when she was desperate and addicted, parts of my childhood were very difficult for me. But God got me through it.

3. When I was twenty-four years old, I sat down at a table to take my own life because I couldn't see past my depression and hopelessness. But God miraculously brought me through it.

4. When my oldest son was almost two years old, and my wife was pregnant with our second son, we felt called to sell everything we had and move to a city with no family, no job, no money, and no place to live to try to start a church. And God brought us through it.

There were several more items on my list, but you get the point. I've had my fair share of days where things looked bleak, but God came through. At that point, it was about three in the morning, and I just lay there in bed reading each memory over and over again.

That list became a memorial.

As I went, God kept reminding me of all the battles he'd already won, and my confidence began to rise. I started saying thank you to God for all the situations he'd brought me through, as we talked about in the previous chapter.

I began to thank God for loving me.

I began to thank God for not giving up on me.

I began to thank God for his Son, who died for me.

I began to thank God for everything on my list, line by line.

And for the first time in a long time, I fell asleep with some confidence, focusing on gratitude instead of fear.

When we woke up the next morning, I brushed my teeth and walked back into our bedroom. Jill came into the room and told me they were all getting ready for the boat ride and that she was going to explain to them that we'd decided to stay here.

"No, you're not."

She looked shocked. "What are you talking about?"

I told her all about how I'd spent the night making a list of the things God had already brought me through. Then I said, "So yeah, I'm a little nervous, but we've been here before, and God never let me down. Let's go take a boat ride!"

This is not just fancy church talk or jargon about theoretical ideas. I'm telling you: you can do the very same thing today. If you're dealing with depression and hopelessness or feel anxiety beginning to attack, *remember to attack back*. Make yourself a list of what God has already brought you through, then look at your current situation and declare out loud: "I've been here before. And I serve an all-knowing, all-powerful God. My God has got this. And because he does, yes I can!"

### List #2: Remember What God Has Promised You

The second thing you need to start remembering is what God promised you. This is way easier said than done. Especially when things get out of control. When times are good, it's easy to talk about God's faithfulness, but when life throws curveballs, we often lose sight of God's promises.

*We can't let that happen.*

During the hardest moments, you need to double down and stand on God's promises all the more. This means you have to make sure you build out systems to remind yourself who God is and who God says you are, even when things get tough.

For your second list, I want you to write out a series of God's promises that you can stand on when things get tough.

I did this a while back. I call the list my war chest.

It's twenty Bible verses that remind me who I am and who God is in every situation. These are the verses I go to when I'm feeling weak, lonely, insecure, afraid, worried, confused, anxious, depressed, or hopeless. These are the verses I read aloud when I get tired of banking on my own opinions and decide to stand on something time-tested and true.

I'm going to share my war chest with you—not because I believe you need to pick the exact same verses for yours but because I think these will get you off on the right foot.

### I AM LOVED

"But God demonstrates his own love for us in this: While we were still sinners, Christ died for us" (Romans 5:8).

### I AM VALUED

"Look at the birds of the air; they do not sow or reap or store away in barns, and yet your heavenly Father feeds them. Are you not much more valuable than they?" (Matthew 6:26).

### I AM ACCEPTED

"Therefore, there is now no condemnation for those who are in Christ Jesus" (Romans 8:1).

### I AM CHOSEN

"For he chose us in him before the creation of the world to be holy and blameless in his sight" (Ephesians 1:4).

### I AM CALLED

"He has saved us and called us to a holy life—not because of anything we have done but because of his own purpose and grace" (2 Timothy 1:9).

### I AM SAFE

"The LORD will keep you from all harm—he will watch over your life" (Psalm 121:7).

### I AM PROTECTED

"But the Lord is faithful, and he will strengthen you and protect you from the evil one" (2 Thessalonians 3:3).

### GOD IS WITH ME

"Have I not commanded you? Be strong and courageous. Do not be afraid; do not be discouraged, for the LORD your God will be with you wherever you go" (Joshua 1:9).

### GOD WILL NEVER LEAVE ME

"And surely I am with you always, to the very end of the age" (Matthew 28:20).

### GOD WILL STRENGTHEN ME

"I can do all things through Him who strengthens me" (Philippians 4:13 NASB).

### GOD WILL GUIDE ME

"Your word is a lamp for my feet, a light on my path" (Psalm 119:105).

### GOD WILL EMPOWER ME

"What, then, shall we say in response to these things? If God is for us, who can be against us?" (Romans 8:31).

### HIS SPIRIT LIVES IN ME

"Do you not know that your bodies are temples of the Holy Spirit, who is in you, whom you have received from God?" (1 Corinthians 6:19).

### GOD IS GREATER

"You, dear children, are from God and have overcome them, because the one who is in you is greater than the one who is in the world" (1 John 4:4).

### I AM MORE THAN A CONQUEROR

"No, in all these things we are more than conquerors through him who loved us" (Romans 8:37).

### NO WEAPON FORMED AGAINST ME SHALL PROSPER

"No weapon formed against you shall prosper" (Isaiah 54:17 NKJV).

### GOD HAS A PLAN WHEN I CAN'T SEE IT

"'For I know the plans I have for you,' declares the LORD, 'plans to prosper you and not to harm you, plans to give you hope and a future'" (Jeremiah 29:11).

### GOD IS WORKING WHEN I CAN'T FEEL IT

"And we know that in all things God works for the good of those who love him, who have been called according to his purpose" (Romans 8:28).

### NOTHING IS IMPOSSIBLE FOR MY GOD

"Jesus looked at them and said, 'With man this is impossible, but with God all things are possible'" (Matthew 19:26).

### I WILL BE VICTORIOUS

"For the LORD your God is the one who goes with you to fight for you against your enemies to give you victory" (Deuteronomy 20:4).

———

This second list is essential.

Feelings will come and go. We will have good days and bad, but God's Word will always be true. Your war chest gives you a firm foundation to stand on when the world is spinning out of control.

Yours doesn't need to look exactly like mine. But feel free to use any or all of it. God gives us so many amazing promises in his Word. Find the ones you need, write them out as your second list, and practice declaring them out loud!

Because remember, anxiety is going to attack, but we can attack back.

When we home in on these two lists—what God has brought us through and what he has promised us—we don't have to wonder if God will take care of us. That's the power of choosing to remember!

Let's make one final list to bring this all together.

## *List #3: Remember God Is Going with You*

Before Joshua led the nation of Israel across the Jordan River, before he witnessed God miraculously stop the flowing water, all he knew was that he had a calling. He knew he had this thing God was leading him to do, and he had no idea how it could possibly work.

Put yourself in Joshua's place for a second:

- My leader and friend just died.
- Everything in life has changed.
- Nothing makes sense.
- I'm scared to death.
- Everyone is looking to me, and I have no idea how to pull this off.

Have you ever felt that way? You've probably never had to lead an entire nation, but we all have our own battles and obstacles standing in front of us.

Which means that even though God said these words to comfort Joshua, we can apply them to our own lives as well. Picture God saying this to you and your loved ones right now: "Be strong and courageous. Do not be afraid; do not be discouraged, for the LORD your God will be with you wherever you go" (Joshua 1:9).

This is so huge! This is not just a promise for Joshua—this is a promise to every single one of us today that applies to what we're dealing with right now. Understanding that the God of the universe goes everywhere we go can begin to push away our anxiety and depression and begin to usher in peace, joy, and freedom like few other things in this world can. Realizing that this applies to us in our lives today is so important in the attacking anxiety process that, later, I'm going to spend an entire chapter unpacking this amazing promise.

When we remember that our heavenly Father is going with us, it changes everything about how we walk, talk, and live our lives day by day.

You don't have to know how tomorrow is going to play out. You don't have to know what's going to happen with the situation you're facing right now. You don't have to understand how the current worry is going to resolve.

All you need to know is your heavenly Father is going with you every step of the way, and *there's nothing in this world he can't handle.*

For your final list, write "God Is Going with Me" at the top.

Then write out all the things that are weighing you down. Seriously. Don't hold back. I'm talking about the real stuff. The biggest ones you can think of.

Now set that list down on a table in front of you and read through it. After that, bring out your first list, the one about everything God has brought you through, and set it on top of your list of worries.

Read that list out loud again.

Finally, bring out your list of what God has promised you and set it on top of both of those lists. Take a second and declare those promises out loud.

Then I just want you to notice how small your third list starts to feel when you realize God is going with you. Your worries and concerns are legitimate, but when you compare them to who God is and everything he's brought you through, they begin to lose their power.

Remember:

1. What God has brought you through
2. What God has promised you
3. God is going with you

Do you see how powerful a memorial can be? Do you see what begins to happen when we take time to start attacking back?

Whatever current storm you are in, God is going to get you through it. He's done it before; he will do it again. We just need to remember where we've been so we can start standing on the truth and attacking back!

When we remember those three things, it helps us focus our attention on our new reality. It allows us to put hopelessness, depression, and anxiety in their proper place: underneath all the things that really matter so we can focus on living out God's calling on our lives.

Anxiety is going to attack, but now you know how to attack back! Through worship, prayer, gratitude, and remembering where God has already taken you, we can attack anxiety, defeat depression, and start to walk in brand-new levels of freedom.

# ASSEMBLING AN ARMY

Before you move on to the next section, there is one final thing you need to start. You have to start asking for help. You have to start assembling an army of friends and family who are ready to fight with you.

If my breakdown on the highway taught me anything, it's that I am not strong enough to get through this life on my own. When I tried, I ended up crying on the side of the road. And the same is true for you. Attacking anxiety is not a solo battle.

So, I'm going to ask: Who is fighting with you?

However, before we talk about assembling this army, we first need to address a bigger problem. If you are anything like me, you try to portray an external picture of yourself that is a lot more put together than what's really there internally.

Sound familiar?

We all do it. It's human nature to want to present ourselves in the best possible light. All too often, we want people to fight for us, but they have no idea what the fight even looks like because we've kept our struggles to ourselves all these years.

You may have the most incredible people in the world surrounding you, ready to fight for you, but if they can't see the Enemy they are fighting, how could they possibly know how to help?

Complete honesty with those you love is a necessary step toward freedom.

The question we need to answer honestly is: Are we willing to let our loved ones in on everything? And I mean *everything*.

## FULLY KNOWN AND FULLY LOVED

At their core, every human being wants to be fully known, fully loved, and fully accepted.

We want to be understood.

We want to be validated.

We just want to know that we are okay.

Unfortunately, none of those things are possible unless we are willing to let people into our lives. If we want to be fully loved, we have to be willing to be fully known.

Depending on the level of anxiety or depression that you (or your loved one) are experiencing, there's a good chance you haven't been able to hide all of it successfully. Unless you are an award-winning actor, it's difficult to hide everything.

So let's be real: We've found a work-around, haven't we? Our strategy is to let our loved ones in just enough to keep them blind to what is actually going on. We tell them we have some anxiety at times or feel a little depressed when things aren't going our way, but then we stop.

I was the master at this for years. I would let people in on just enough of my anxiety and depression to throw them off the scent so I didn't have to show them the depths of it. I told everyone (including our church) that I occasionally struggled with anxiety and depression, but *nobody* knew how bad it was.

We are okay with letting people in on 90 percent of our struggles, but it's the last 10 percent, the real dark places, deep pain, and desperate thoughts, that we are too embarrassed to ever say out loud. That's the stuff we consider humiliating. That's the stuff we want to take to our graves.

We all feel so much shame around that last 10 percent because no one ever wants to talk about it. Then what happens is we begin to feel like we might be the only ones who experience it, at least at the level that we do. The Enemy loves it when we feel isolated like that because then he can convince us to shove down the dark stuff and never tell a soul.

We feel guilty for having our 10 percent.

We feel shame because of it.

We feel broken for experiencing it.

This strategy makes sense. Who in their right mind would ever want to tell those they love the most about the deepest, darkest parts of their soul? Especially if we believe at some level that we are at fault for our mental illnesses. And so, instead of letting people in and finding freedom, the Enemy convinces us to continue suffering silently.

At least that's what happened to me.

# SUFFERING SILENTLY

The truth about my breakdown on the side of the road is that it was a long time coming. The problem was, nobody could see the warning signs because nobody knew how bad my situation was—not even my wife. Sure, she knew I struggled, but she didn't know the depths of the struggle.

I hadn't slept well in years. And every time I sought professional medical help, I was just prescribed more Ambien. I took ten milligrams every night for years. At one point, I remember saying to a doctor, "Hey, this feels like a lot of Ambien. Is this unhealthy?" And I was told that I could take that much for the rest of my life.

My body had grown so accustomed to it that it wasn't even coming close to helping me get to sleep, but I knew if I didn't take it, I'd literally be up for the rest of the night.

And my family had no idea.

They slept fine. But I would stay up all night trying to numb my brain with my phone, computer, and sleeping pills. I did everything I could to keep my mind occupied because whenever there were quiet moments, my mind was at its worst. I'd lay in bed and feel so guilty for still having anxiety at my age. I'd feel ashamed for still feeling depressed even though God had given me so many blessings. That's where the dark thoughts would begin to surface, my worry would be at its highest, and my self-worth would be at its lowest.

Rather than talk to someone about it, I would try to numb it. I'd turn to even more sleeping pills, binge even more TV, and scroll a bit longer, all in an unsuccessful attempt to fall asleep without having to deal with the darkness in my mind.

And my loved ones had no idea.

My days weren't much better. Every week, I had to speak to thousands of people all around the world. I knew they all needed some good news, and I wanted so badly to appear confident for them, so I would obsess over every word, hoping that no one would realize how afraid I was.

My nights may have been *restless*, but my days felt *reckless*. I was anxious all the time and was beginning to have more and more panic attacks. Airplanes, cars, and elevators (you know, all the day-to-day activities that you can't really avoid) would send me into humiliating spirals of panic every time.

And my friends had no idea.

I thought I was sheltering the people I loved by not telling them the depth of my issues. But what I had to learn the hard way is that I was building invisible walls between me and my wife, my closest friends, and my boys.

I had people in my life who wanted to help, but I wasn't giving them an opportunity to try. I wasn't giving them a chance to love me. I thought I was being strong by not telling them, but instead I was, in essence, saying I was only going to allow a certain level of closeness because there was a part of me I didn't believe they should see.

I wanted to be fully loved, but I wasn't willing to be fully known. Instead of letting people in, I was suffering silently.

## WHAT ABOUT YOU?

Unfortunately, there are so many people doing the same thing—keeping their pain to themselves. And it's not their fault. A lot of people are trained from a young age to bury their burdens and push down their pain. And then, years later, they realize they don't even understand their own struggles.

*If I don't understand my own pain, there's no chance anyone else will ever be able to, right?*

That's the thought that plagues so many of us. We believe others will think we are crazy and have no idea how to help. So instead of giving them a chance, we lock up our pain and create a prison inside our own minds that we have to deal with for the rest of our lives.

Please hear me: that is a lie from the pit of hell.

The more you start talking about this, the more you're going to find out there are people all around you who are dealing with the same thing. A whole bunch of us are all keeping the same secret.

This book is about freedom, so let me set you free. I know the thoughts you've already had when it comes to sharing this stuff because I had the same ones. Not only are you *not* the only one who deals with anxiety and depression, but you're also not the only one who deals with the same excuses or mental roadblocks that keep you from wanting to share this stuff with the people in your life.

Let me guess, that self-justification goes something like this: *Well, I don't want people to know how broken I am because I don't want to let them down. I'm afraid of the embarrassment and humiliation that will come with it. I would never want people to think less of me. Maybe this chapter isn't for me; I'm just going to keep this stuff to myself. After all, I would never want to be a burden to other people. They are all so busy. They've got their own problems to deal with. They don't need to help carry my stuff. And besides, if people in my life really knew how broken I am, they might not love me. They might leave me. I could lose my job. I could lose a relationship.*

Did that strike a chord? Let's take it down another level and get to the utter core: *I feel guilty for feeling this way. I am ashamed of myself for feeling this way. And deep down inside, I somehow blame myself for this. So yeah, I better just keep quiet.*

If any of that sounds familiar, I'm with you. I know how this stuff plays out in our minds because I'm well accustomed to all those lies. And remember, that's exactly what those are: *lies.*

I can't tell you how much freedom you will begin to experience when you start sharing your brokenness with loved ones in your life. Words can't describe how great it feels to shine some light on the dark places in your soul. It feels a lot like freedom. And you deserve to feel that freedom.

The worst way to suffer is by yourself. So, I'll ask you again: Who is fighting with you? And do they know the depths of your struggle?

Think about it this way: the people closest to you in life can't fight for you if they don't know you're in a fight. James 5:16 says, "Therefore confess your sins to each other and pray for each other so that you may be healed."

According to the Bible, if I bring you my worst and you bring me your worst, but then we come together in prayer, miraculous healing becomes possible in Jesus' name!

That's what we need when it comes to our anxiety and depression. We need the miraculous power of God to get involved.

Step one is to get it all out, so share the real you with someone who will pray for you. There's freedom that takes place when you can stop hiding. There's a peace that begins to creep in when you know you can stop pretending around certain people and just be real. Be you.

Once I allowed the people close to me to begin fighting along with me, it changed the entire war. I stopped waking up alone with my own thoughts, wondering how I would survive on my own, because I knew I had an army fighting along with me.

# ENLIST THE RIGHT PEOPLE

Bringing my struggles into the light didn't magically fix everything, but it did remind me that I wasn't alone. Even in my darkest hours, I knew I always had my closest friends a phone call away. I'm telling you, fighting alongside people changed the entire battle for me. And it will do the same for you. I'm begging you, let some people fight alongside you.

All those months of counseling were challenging, but what got me through was knowing that I wasn't fighting by myself. I'd wake up every morning with a text from my wife full of Scripture verses about peace, about joy, about God being with me today, about God fighting my battles and comforting me when I'm struggling. My friends started sending me encouragement, leaving me voicemails, and traveling out to see me so I didn't have to be alone with my thoughts.

Having people in the trenches with me changed everything.

It's time to start getting real with those closest to you. Let them know that you need their help. Just be honest. Explain to them how bad your mental health has become. Then let them know that you've realized anxiety and depression are not things you want to fight alone, and ask them if they would consider fighting along with you. Open up and ask:

- Can I call you when it gets really bad?
- Would you pray for me?

- Would you ask me how I'm doing occasionally?

If we are going to attack anxiety, we are going to need an army. So let's end this entire section by getting super practical. Below, there are five different categories of people. I encourage you to examine these areas and ask yourself if they apply to you and from which categories you should enlist people to begin fighting the battle alongside you.

Don't skip this exercise. If I didn't have these people in my life when I hit rock bottom, I'm not sure I'd still be here. It's time to start assembling an army that will help us attack back!

## Category #1: Family

If you're married, your spouse is most likely the first person you should tell. Jill was my first enlistee, and I'm so glad she was. I never really knew how strong my wife was and how much she loved me until I shared the deep, dark parts of my life with her. Our marriage went to new depths.

If you feel embarrassed about telling your spouse after all these years, remember it took me twenty years to finally let my wife in. There is no time like the present. I'm telling you, we've never been more in love and a better team than we are right now.

When I told my sister Lorrie how bad it was, she packed up her things and moved across the country to be with us. She can work remotely, so she moved in with us to help the kids while I was at counseling. I don't know what we would have done without her.

Parents, let's talk for a second. Your kids aren't stupid; they probably already know. They see us struggle, and they want freedom for us too. The night I finally told my boys about my struggles, I was a mess. Through tears, I told them how it was getting worse and that I needed to go to some extensive counseling out of state. I hated the thought of missing a few months of their football games, basketball games, and just life in general. And I was worried they were going to be shocked.

But my son looked at me with a smile and said, "Dad, I've watched you deal with anxiety my whole life. I love you. Go to counseling." My honesty with my boys has brought us closer together as a family than we've ever been before.

You don't have to tell the whole world what's going on with you, but you need to tell someone in this world. And your family is a great place to start. Once the people closest to you are in the battle with you, sharing with the next level of people in your life will get easier and easier. I'm telling you—you can do this!

## Category #2: Friends

After you begin letting your family in on your struggles, the next step is to tell your friends. Ever since I came clean to my friend BZ, he has never stopped sending me encouraging texts and Bible verses and just randomly calling to tell me he loves me, believes in me, and is fighting for me.

My long-time, trusted friend Scott has a prayer life like few people I've ever known. He's the person I call when I am in my absolute darkest hours. There have been a few nights where I've felt suicidal. Each time, he's sat on the phone with me, praying for me until I started to feel God's peace set in.

As I mentioned earlier, Jimmy and Irene Rollins flew across the country to sit with Jill and me. But that was just the beginning. They call, text, and video chat frequently to remind us that we are not going through this alone.

Pastor Chris was a lifesaver for me.

Pastor Craig and Pastor Amy are two of the busiest, most influential, and sought-after people that I know. But no matter where they were or what they were doing, they constantly made time to check in on me and Jill, to encourage, support, pray for, and love us. I don't know where we'd be today without them.

Pastor Dino, Layne, Micahn, Mayo, and Jeremy have been incredible. Ronnie, Andrew, Jordan and the rest of the team at Red Rocks Church have supported me in ways I never even knew were possible. Our worship team wrote and recorded songs of encouragement for me. Our church family has embraced me and all my imperfections with open arms. I love them all so much! The list goes on and on of the friends in my life who made my healing journey a reality. I never would've made it alone. I'm telling you, *anxiety is not a solo battle.*

If your friends don't get to know who you really are, you don't get to see if they're really your ride-or-die friends. And once mine knew how bad it was, they went to war with me in ways I never expected. It changed the game. Start enlisting friends who

- will pray for you,
- will be there to hang out when things get bad, and
- will continuously remind you of the things we seem to forget in the middle of anxiety or depression and push you closer to the presence and promises of God.

## Category #3: Church

The next step is to tell your church. There is a pressure in churches to pretend like you have it all together; I know it all too well. But that pressure is a lie that we need to call out. The church is a place for imperfect people to pursue a perfect God together as a community. Start taking advantage of that community.

For me, the church is my place of employment. So it was a little scary. I was nervous about what people may think of me. The same may be true for you. But when I came clean, I can't tell you how freeing it was. They just needed to know. Not for their sake as much as for mine. Pretending is exhausting. If you want peace instead of anxiety, set yourself free from your secrets. Talk to people in your church. If you don't have one, I would encourage you to try finding one you like. Join a group or whatever your church offers for community and find some people who will surround you and fight for you.

## Category #4: Doctors

The next person on your list will likely be a doctor or primary care provider you trust. I'm not a doctor, so I won't pretend like I know what I'm talking about with medicine. Instead, here's my best advice: find a doctor you feel *comfortable* talking to and *confident* listening to.

When it comes to plans and prescriptions, everyone's situation is different. I needed some doctors who not only knew anxiety and depression but who also were willing to sit with me and listen to my circumstances. Once I found the right doctors, they helped me get off the unhealthy stuff and put together a real plan toward freedom. Once we had a plan, they got me dialed in on the right medications, and it has made a world of difference.

### Category #5: Counselors

The final person I want you to consider is a counselor. I spent my whole adult life pretending my past abuse and hurts didn't affect me. I wasn't afraid of counseling as much as I was afraid of being the guy who needed counseling. So I convinced myself that I didn't need it.

But I was wrong.

Grief counseling and trauma therapy set me free in ways that I can't even put into words. Once I started, I began experiencing freedom from bondage I didn't realize I had. I still go to a counselor once a week, and I'll probably never stop. It's so good for me, and I bet it would be for you too.

If talking to someone like that sounds scary or makes you feel weak, you are not alone. That's exactly how I felt. But there is real beauty and healing in realizing we were created to do life together, leaning on others in times of need. I challenge you to step out of your comfort zone, talk to a trained counselor/doctor/therapist, and just see what sort of freedom might lie on the other side of that decision for you.

# DON'T HOLD BACK

How did you do on that list?

For each category that applies to your situation, do you have someone there who is fighting along with you? If not, it's time to start asking for help. It's time to start assembling your army.

And remember, I'm talking about letting people in on everything. You may have glanced over all those categories and thought,

*Well, I've already got friends and family I've let in.* Great! But now my challenge to you is to let them in *all the way.*

Share the last 10 percent. Tell them how bad it gets. They can't go to battle with you if they don't know you're in a war.

Let them all the way in!

Nobody knew about my sleeping pills. They didn't know just how much stress I had or how poorly I was managing it. They didn't know about my misery on the inside. They didn't know the darkness of my thought life. They weren't aware that there were times I wanted to end it all.

Nobody knew.

My pride and fear of humiliation wouldn't allow the truth to come out. I was so convinced it would cause them to think less of me. But the part that I didn't see coming is that when I finally let them in, they all respected me more—even our church staff—which was really shocking to me. And once they finally knew the truth, they actually knew how to be praying for me.

Anxiety is a battle we can win, but it's not a battle we can win on our own. In the next section, we will talk about the things we need to stop doing on our journey to freedom. But first, it's time to start letting some people go to war with you.

Just tell them what is really going on.

Let them know that previously you've let them part of the way in, but now you are giving them access to the whole thing—to the depths of your anxiety and depression. We were created to pursue the plans of God with the people of God, so get the right people in your corner, let them in on everything, and watch what happens!

# Part 3
# *STOP*

# PRETENDING YOU'RE OKAY

As we enter a new section of this book, let's do a quick recap. Anxiety, depression, and hopelessness are real. They affect everybody differently, and they often come out of the blue. Whether it's you or a loved one who is struggling with these things, the fact is they are a very real part of our broken world.

But we can fight back.

The first step is to know three things:

1. You are not crazy.
2. You are not alone.
3. This will end.

However, knowledge is only part of the battle. If we want to win this war, there aren't just things we need to *know*—there are also things we have to *start*. At some point, we have to decide that enough is enough, put our foot down, and get to work. Anxiety and depression will attack, but eventually, we need to make the conscious decision to attack back. God has so much more for us, and the day we decide to start fighting for it, the battle for abundant life begins.

The secret to winning any war is equipping ourselves with the correct weapons. Remember the four ways of attacking back that we've already looked at:

1. *Worship.* When you consistently spend time worshiping God, things will begin to change.
2. *Pray.* There is no right or wrong way to talk to God. Tell him about what you are feeling. Speak to him about the things going on in your head and your heart. Ask him for what you need and thank him for what he's already done. He is our loving Father who just wants to talk to us.
3. *Remind yourself of all the victories in the past.* When your heart starts feeling heavy with depression or your mind begins racing with anxious thoughts, the next way to attack back is to actively and intentionally remind yourself of what God has already promised you and already brought you through and that he's with you right now.
4. *Assemble an army to fight with you.* Surround yourself with people who love you enough to be in the fight with you, and then stop hiding from them the depths of your depression and the scattered feelings of your anxiety.

Now it's time to talk about what to *stop*. When it comes to battling anxiety and depression, there are some dos, but there are also a lot of don'ts. This section is about the don'ts. It's about the things in your life that you need to get rid of. We've been talking about all the things we need to add to our lives, but now let's talk about the things we need to subtract. It's time to take a stand for your freedom, draw a line in the sand, and eliminate all the unhealthy habits in your life that are causing anxiety and depression.

The problem is that you may not know what those things are. When my life was spiraling, I didn't know why. Sometimes it is difficult to identify the items in our own lives that need to go. If it were easy to know what needs to go, we would've gotten rid of those things by now.

That's why rock bottom can sometimes be helpful. Rock bottom forces us to stop the show. It's where we realize we aren't good enough, strong enough, or smart enough to overcome anxiety or depression on our own. It reveals what needs to change in our lives and forces us to face the reality of our issues and get desperate enough to do something about them.

To help identify some of the things you need to stop, I'd like to start by sharing a conversation I had with a good friend of mine about his rock bottom. We've both had to learn these lessons the hard way, and we are sharing our experiences in the hopes that you decide to learn these lessons the easy way.

## A NECESSARY ENDING

A week or so into my time in Alabama, I felt like I was beginning to make some progress. My wife and I were going into the war room every single day, battling with worship and prayer. I was making my lists and reminding myself of all the things God had already brought me through. Plus, I had already had a couple of honest and open conversations with loved ones and people close to me.

But something was still missing.

And it wasn't until I sat down for a conversation with a man named Dino that I knew what that something was.

By the time I hung out with Dino, my new pastor friend, I was done trying to cover up how screwed up I was. I was well past the point of no return and had no energy left to try to hide it. Instead, I took the opposite approach and told him everything.

I told him about losing it in my truck.

All the anxiety and depression I had been dealing with for years.

How overwhelmed I felt at work and just with life in general.

I even told him how hopeless I felt at times that things would ever get any better.

That's quite a way to start a conversation with a new friend, but I had been trying to keep up an appearance for years, and the only fruit I was feeling was exhaustion, so instead, I just let it fly.

Dino listened patiently, letting me get it all out before interjecting. When I finished, I figured he'd be looking for the exit. But instead, he did one of the best things you could ever do for somebody struggling with this stuff: he began to tell me about his own struggles.

He told me about a time in his life when his career was at an all-time high. He was being asked to speak at large churches all around the country and conferences all around the world. He had never been so successful. On paper, he was living the dream.

However, what no one would've guessed in a million years was that as his career was on the rise, his mental health was quickly falling.

He began to tell me about all his anxiety, his fight with depression, and the heaviness of his hopelessness. Then at one point, he told me it got so bad that he didn't want to keep on living. When his career was at a high point, his mental health was at a low point.

Dino hit rock bottom.

And it was at that moment he realized something profound. God could have stopped him from going so low, but he didn't. God allowed him to hit rock bottom.

Think about that for a second. Why would such a loving God allow him to go so low? Because rock bottom was the place Dino realized just how desperate the situation was. Rock bottom was the place Dino decided things needed to change. Rock bottom was the place Dino knew he had to stop pretending he was okay. He couldn't continue living this way—it was time to cut some things out of his life.

What was shocking to me was that Dino said rock bottom was the place he realized just how much God loved him. God loved him enough to let him get to the end of his own strength so that he could realize how much he needed to rely on God's strength.

As Dino continued to explain his rock bottom experience to me, I knew God was speaking to me about mine. Dino told me rock bottom is where we stop denying that we have a problem and stop pretending that we have enough power to overcome that problem on our own. He told me there is no more use for our pride or our feeble attempts at pulling ourselves up by our bootstraps at rock bottom. And then he said something I'll never forget: "God showed me it was time for a necessary ending."

*A necessary ending.*

Those three words resonated with me deeply. I wasn't quite sure what he meant, but I knew it was for me. He could tell I was a bit puzzled, so he went on to explain that he had some unhealthy things in his life that had to go. Some of them had only been happening for a small amount of time, but others had been there for several years. And each one of them was making him anxious and pulling him into bouts of depression. Rock bottom revealed how deadly they were and that they needed to change.

Some of the things were obvious; they were staring him right in the eye. Other things were harder to see. But regardless, one thing was clear as day: the way he had been living life wasn't going to work anymore. He needed to change, and he needed that change to begin immediately. He knew the change wasn't going to be easy, and it wasn't going to be immediate. But he also knew the change was going to be inevitable.

This was *a necessary ending.*

At that point in the conversation, Dino had a huge smile on his face. He explained that as difficult as his necessary ending had been, he had also never felt so free. He had never had more peace or experienced more joy because he was finally ready to stop the things in his life that weren't supposed to be there so that he could step up and become the person God was calling him to be.

He went on to admit that he doesn't recognize his old self anymore. The transformation was real. The freedom, the victory, and the peace in his life today all began when he realized something had to change. It was time for certain things to go, other things to change, and a few things to be put to death once and for all.

As I sat across from my new friend, I could feel something begin to shift in my soul. "Shawn," he said confidently, "that's exactly where God has you right now. God loves you too much to let you keep going the way you are. You're at a necessary ending."

As I sat there listening to Dino, I knew his story was really my story, and I realized that I was going to have to stop pretending. Because I had been pretending for a long time. I think that when we face difficult things and don't know how to fix them or what to do about them, one of our natural instincts is to just pretend the difficult thing isn't there. We treat ourselves like little kids. When my three boys were little, we played peekaboo. They would put their hands over their eyes and pretend that they couldn't see me. Or I would put my hands over my eyes and pretend I couldn't see them. And then we would quickly remove our hands from our eyes and say, "Peekaboo!" We'd all laugh and act surprised, as if simply putting our hands over our eyes and pretending that the other person wasn't there meant that they actually weren't.

I realized I was doing that with my anxiety and depression. They would pop up out of nowhere sometimes and scare me—even wreck me for hours or days at a time. But as soon as the feelings passed, I would just put my hands over my eyes and pretend my anxiety and depression weren't really there instead of acknowledging the reality of my situation and seeking out help. I interacted with my family, my friends, people at our church—all people who would have loved an opportunity to help me—with my hands over my eyes, pretending I was okay, pretending I was doing well in life and was never in need of help.

My pretending to be okay became a lifestyle. I knew deep down I was headed in the wrong direction; I knew it was getting worse. I knew I needed help. But I was deathly afraid to share my struggles with anyone around me. So I just kept pretending. And, somehow, I thought if I pretended well enough, maybe it would all go away.

Do you ever do that in your life? Know you need to face a person, a situation, an issue, but the pain it might cause or the discomfort you might feel seems overwhelming, so you just pretend the issue isn't there? You put your hands over your eyes and act like everything is somehow going to be okay? The problem is, eventually you remove your hands from your eyes and discover that whatever was there, is still there.

Dino's story made me realize that I couldn't keep pretending my anxiety and depression hadn't reached debilitating levels.

It didn't matter that I was a pastor; it didn't matter that we had a large staff. It didn't matter that I was responsible for a lot of people; it didn't matter that God had put me in a place of leadership in my family and in my career—none of that mattered. What mattered was accepting my reality: I was experiencing very real and debilitating levels of anxiety and depression, and they were stealing the peace and joy and freedom from my life. It was time to do something about it. I had to stop pretending and start fighting back.

I'd known this that day on the side of the road, but I hadn't known what to do about it. I'd told my wife over and over, "I can't live this way. I can't live this way." But what I was really saying—I just hadn't realized it at the time—was, "I can't pretend anymore!" Because every now and then, my hands would come down from my eyes and I would see that my anxiety and depression were still there. And it was killing me.

My experience on the side of the road was the beginning of a new journey that has led me to more peace, joy, and freedom than I ever thought I would experience. But the starting point, without a doubt, was realizing I had to stop pretending that:

- I was okay when I wasn't;
- I had dealt with the past when I hadn't;
- I was strong enough to get through this stuff on my own;
- I didn't need God's help;
- I didn't need other people's help;
- I was going to be okay the way I was.

My talk with Dino about a necessary ending was the nail in the coffin to my pretending. I realized I had to put pretending to death. I needed to acknowledge the severity of what I was experiencing and decide to do something about it. I was ready to stop pretending and start fighting.

## ARE YOU READY TO STOP PRETENDING?

Are you trying to live out your life with your hands over your eyes? Are you in need of a necessary ending in your life? Maybe you've been pretending you're okay for too long and it's time to stop. God loves you too much to let you stay stuck. It's okay to admit you're not okay.

Let's be honest: some of us need to fall all the way down before we will actually get desperate enough to do something about our descent. Because at our lowest points we are ready to surrender; at our lowest points we are ready to walk away from everything. At our lowest points we are ready for *a necessary ending*.

That conversation with Dino changed the trajectory of my life, and I'm praying this section will do the same for you. If you (or a loved one) are struggling with anxiety or dealing with depression, let that phrase speak to you the same way it spoke to me.

This is your moment.

It's time for a change.

It's time to put some things to death so that you can begin to truly live.

God has brought you to a necessary ending.

Jesus put it like this: "Let me make this clear: A single grain of wheat will never be more than a single grain of wheat unless it drops into the ground and dies. Because then it sprouts and produces a great harvest of wheat—all because one grain died" (John 12:24 TPT).

Do you see what Jesus was saying?

There are times that we need to put something in our lives to death so that we can begin to truly live! That's exactly where I was. And there's a real good chance that's where you or a loved one is right now.

This section is about learning to stop the things that cause us anxiety and depression so that we can start to truly live. I'm going to share some very practical things that many of us will deal with. My challenge to you is to do some self-reflection. As you read these next few chapters, ask yourself these two questions:

1. Are there things in my life that I do consistently that cause my anxiety to go up?
2. Are there things that are in my control that cause me to spiral into a state of depression?

Like we talked about in the last chapter, if you want to really get some good answers, invite your family, friends, church, doctor, and counselor in on the conversation. Ask them to help you see your blind spots.

And most importantly, invite God to go through this section with you. In fact, take a second to do that right now by praying this simple prayer:

*God, I trust you. Thank you for walking with me through all of this. As I read, would you reveal to me the things in my life that I need to stop? Help me see the things that are adding to my anxiety and depression, and give me the strength to eliminate them from my life.*

Like anything worthwhile in life, this section is going to take work. But trust me, you can do this. You can stop pretending. And one day, you will look back on your life and be so thankful that you did. That's Dino's story. That's my story. And this can be your story too. When we stop pretending we're okay, it opens the door to a journey that will lead to more peace, joy, and freedom than we ever thought possible. You'll be so grateful that God loved you enough to bring you to a necessary ending.

# HOLDING ON TO UNFORGIVENESS

The second thing we need to stop is holding on to unforgiveness. Every one of us has pain in our past, and unless we do the difficult work to face it and forgive it, it will continue to fuel our anxiety and depression.

During my seven-week stint of inpatient treatment, I met with several counselors. Each one brought a slightly different angle to the table. But I'll never forget the very first counselor I met with on day one.

His name was Robert, and he asked me a few simple questions and then sat back and quietly listened to me as I cried hysterically for about fifteen minutes. I just kept telling him how bad the anxiety was while he nodded his head. Then he pulled out a notebook and ripped a page out.

"Okay," he said, pulling a pen out of his pocket. "Let's make a list of your grievances."

"I'm sorry?" I said, feeling a bit frustrated—as if he hadn't listened to a single word I'd said.

"It's time to list out your grievances," he continued a little too casually. "Who in life has hurt you?"

That seemed like an odd place to start. At the time, I didn't think I was in counseling to talk about my past; I wanted to talk about how I could have peace in the present and set myself up to thrive in the future. What I didn't realize is that sometimes to move forward, we first have to go back and heal from past pain.

I didn't really want to make a list of grievances, but since I had come all this way, I decided to play along. I listed off a handful of names of people who had hurt me. I told him who they were, what they had done, and how bad it hurt.

"Okay," he continued. "It's time to learn to forgive."

## PAST PAIN

Remember that list I told you about in the last section of all the things God has brought me through? Well, just because God brings you through something doesn't mean you come out of it without a few bumps and bruises. My past caused me a lot of pain. And as much as I tried to deny it, that pain was one of the root causes of my anxiety and depression.

In case you forgot what I'm talking about, here's a refresher:

- My biological father left me before I was born. I've never met him and have dealt with abandonment issues, unanswered questions, and pain my whole life.

- My mom left me on a stranger's porch when I was a baby and jumped off a bridge (and survived).
- My mom developed a heroin addiction, and I went through some very painful seasons of life as a result of her struggles.
- My past is littered with emotional, physical, and even sexual abuses.
- I also entered a life of drug abuse as a young adult that led to anxiety, depression, and suicidal thoughts.

There's a lot more, but the point is: I have a past. You do too. And so do your loved ones. Believe it or not, the pain from your past is affecting your present.

For as long as I can remember, I've either tried to forget what I went through growing up or pretended it did not affect me. But neither of those strategies work. Suppressing pain, pretending it never happened, or minimizing the effects of it will only set you up for more anxiety and depression in your life.

It turns out, my pride was the first thing that needed to come to a necessary ending. I needed to stop holding on to unforgiveness. I needed to stop pretending my past wasn't affecting my present. I needed to stop ignoring it and trying to push it down. I needed to stop trying to outrun it. It was time to admit that I needed healing.

And maybe the same is true for you today.

Remember, one of the reasons I'm writing this book is because I realize you probably don't have the luxury of running off to seven weeks of counseling. So, I'm passing on as much insight as I can from my own experience. However, this book is not a substitute for counseling. You should absolutely talk to a professional if you can. As the Proverb says, "Where there is no counsel, the people fall; But in the multitude of counselors there is safety" (11:14 NKJV).

Working through past pain is not easy, but it is possible. One of the most powerful and practical ways to start is to learn the art of forgiveness.

Robert was right.

Forgiveness is the starting point for healing past wounds and became one of the main lessons I had to work through during my time in counseling. Holding on to unforgiveness requires so much anxiety-producing energy. We do it because we think we have the right—and we do—but it causes us a lot of anxiety and depression in the process. Imagine how much precious energy we could save if we could learn to let go.

Holding on to unforgiveness is like keeping your hand on a hot stove and then wondering why you are in so much pain. If you saw me do that, you'd plead with me to just move my hand. I care about you enough to tell you to do the same. It's time to take your hand off the stove. It's time to let go of the bitterness and to heal.

But if you've ever tried to let go of bitterness, you know how tricky it can be. Forgiveness is not easy, but the results are profound.

Let's learn to forgive together.

## TIME TO FORGIVE

At this point, you may feel like we've strayed from the path a bit. *Isn't this a book about anxiety and depression? Why are we talking about forgiveness?*

But nothing could be further from the truth.

If you want peace, you have to stop pretending about your past. You have to *face it* and *forgive it*. And that's not just my opinion. Scripture says, "Finally, brothers and sisters, rejoice! Strive for full restoration, encourage one another, be of one mind, live in peace. And the God of love and peace will be with you" (2 Corinthians 13:11). According to the Bible, the forgiveness process is the starting point for peace. And although forgiveness might sound horrific right now, I bet peace sounds pretty amazing. And that's what we're after here!

Forgiveness ushers in peace.

And peace ushers out anxiety.

When Robert told me it was time to forgive, I was angry. I wanted this guy to fix my anxiety, not lecture me on forgiveness. He could tell I was bothered, so in his calm counseling voice, he explained how my unforgiveness was forcing me to stay chained to the very people who had hurt me. My bitterness was giving them permission to continue hurting me on a daily basis. Doing the hard work of forgiving would set me free.

That made a lot of sense.

However, I had no idea where to start, so he walked me through the process of doing the work of forgiveness. I want to take you through the same steps. Forgiveness didn't come easy. This is something I had to work on every day. Slowly but surely, I began to separate myself from the past hurts in my life, and as I did, my anxiety and depression began losing their grip, and peace began to creep in.

I believe the same is going to happen for you. As we walk through these five steps, I'll ask you the same question Robert asked me: Who is one person who has hurt you in the past? Bring that person to mind and see if you can start to forgive.

## *Step #1: Accept What Happened*

The first thing Robert told me to do was realize the weight of what had happened. He told me to stop denying the pain and face it. He gave me permission to acknowledge how bad it hurt. Then he told me to think about how much that moment had affected my life since.

If you want to *forgive it*, you first have to *feel it*.

Do not minimize or deny the pain. Let yourself feel all the emotions that come with it and accept that the pain has negatively affected your life.

## *Step #2: Pray for Them*

The next step is to pray for the person who wronged you. If reading that sentence made you want to chuck this book across the room, I know the feeling. When Robert got to step two, I almost walked out of the room. Praying for the very person who wronged you feels counterintuitive. And it is. But then again, so is forgiveness. It may not make sense, but it will change your life. That's why Jesus told us, "Love your enemies and pray for those who persecute you" (Matthew 5:44).

Jesus knew how prone we'd be to hold on to bitterness, so he gave us the key to letting go—prayer. Spend some time praying for them. If you're like me, even on my most spiritual days, praying for someone who's hurt me just feels overwhelming. I can hardly force myself to say anything nice or hopeful about them out loud. And what I really feel like doing is praying that God would do something to them that, well, is probably going in the opposite direction of what Jesus meant. If you've ever felt that way, don't worry; I'll give you a forgiveness prayer near the end of the chapter to help get you started.

## Step #3: Let Go

Humans have an innate desire to repay evil with evil. When someone wrongs us, it's natural to want to harm them back. But as we learned in kindergarten, two wrongs don't make a right. Or if you want something more concrete, the Bible says it like this:

> Do not repay anyone evil for evil. Be careful to do what is right in the eyes of everyone. If it is possible, as far as it depends on you, live at peace with everyone. Do not take revenge, my dear friends, but leave room for God's wrath, for it is written: "It is mine to avenge; I will repay," says the Lord. (Romans 12:17–19)

This is a big one. The day you let go of needing to repay someone for what they did to you, something will break. Bitterness will lose its grip, and forgiveness will begin to feel possible. For me, I had to start saying it out loud to God. "Okay, I'm letting go of my desire to punish them. I'm letting go of my desire to get even." They were more statements of faith than true feelings in the moment—but it was a start.

## Step #4: Make the Conscious Decision to Forgive

Once you've acknowledged the pain, prayed for them, and let go of the desire to repay evil with evil, it's time to make the conscious decision to forgive. Remember, forgiveness does not come naturally to us; we have to override the system and decide that we will forgive them for all the hurt and pain they've caused.

For some of your situations, it may not be smart (or safe) to have any direct contact with that person. If that's you, don't reach out to them. You can forgive from afar. But if it is safe to reach out, there is something powerful about telling them you forgive them, love them, and are finding healing from any pain they caused.

### Step #5: Work to Reconcile

This final step is only applicable if they show true repentance for the way they hurt you. Repentance doesn't mean just saying sorry—it means changing your actions. It's one thing to apologize; it's another thing to start taking actions in the right direction. If the person who hurt you is genuinely sorry and seeking to reconcile, be open to reconciling with them.

If there is true change on their part, start by slowly working to build back mutual trust, honor, respect, and understanding. If that goes well, you can gradually work on reestablishing a relationship.

Forgiveness is a complicated topic. Simply going through those five steps once may not do the trick, but if you continue to work through each of those steps each day, you'll begin to let go of bitterness and forgive. As you do, you'll notice wounds from your past starting to heal.

# FORGIVENESS VERSUS FELLOWSHIP

One day, I was struggling with the concept of forgiveness. I was in a session with a counselor—let's call him Steve—and I was hesitant to forgive a few people from my past. I kept feeling like if I forgave, I'd be letting them entirely off the hook. As if my forgiveness made what they did okay. People don't always change, so I was worried that if I forgave, I'd be opening myself up to them hurting me again.

I bet you've had similar thoughts. You may even be thinking that right now as I encourage you to forgive. So I asked Steve if forgiveness meant I had to let that person back into my life, and his answer was super helpful.

"Forgive the analogy," he said with a smile. "It's a bit on the crazy side, but it'll help you understand my point. If you hire a babysitter but then find out that babysitter not only chased the children around the house but was an ax murderer in his past, you are going to be furious. You can put in the work to forgive, but you probably aren't going to invite him over for Thanksgiving dinner."

Something about that ridiculous analogy clicked for me. There is a massive difference between *forgiveness* and *fellowship*. The difference has a lot to do with the other person's response (which you can't control). Forgiveness depends on you, but their response is on them.

Everyone deserves forgiveness, but if they don't repent or change, they don't deserve fellowship.

Forgive everyone but only have fellowship with the people who have earned your trust. You can be quick to forgive but slow to trust. Forgiveness brings peace and freedom into your life, but fellowship should only happen if:

1. they repent fully and show they are changing;
2. there is mutual trust, honor, and respect;
3. they are willing to take steps toward repairing the relationship.

Protect your circle. If they aren't willing to take all of those steps, don't waste your energy trying to rebuild the relationship. Reconciliation isn't possible—they aren't ready yet. But if they are, and you feel comfortable with it, you can slowly begin rebuilding the relationship.

Put in the hard work to forgive, but remember, *forgiveness* and *fellowship* are two entirely different things.

# THE FORGIVENESS PRAYER

Forgiveness takes a lot of work. It's like a muscle you have to train. One of the best ways to work that muscle is through prayer. As we've discussed, God wants to talk to you about everything, so why not speak to him about the bitterness you are still holding on to?

If you've never done anything like that, let me walk you through the process. Start by owning your unforgiveness. God already knows about it anyway; you may as well come clean. Just tell God that you are now aware that you've been holding on to bitterness and that you are ready to repent. Declare that you are ready to get rid of all hurt, anger, and bitterness so that you can finally forgive in Jesus' name. Thank God for healing the wounds that the original incident caused and declare that you are giving up the right to judge and punish.

When I do this, it sounds something like this:

> *God, I'm ready to stop pretending like pain in my past is not affecting my present. Please forgive me for holding on to unforgiveness. Today, I declare I am getting rid of this unforgiveness and letting go of this hurt and anger. I completely forgive _____ in Jesus' name, and I thank you that you are healing these wounds that were inflicted. I thank you that*

*you are making me whole and setting me free. And I declare
that I am giving up my right to judge or punish this person. I
completely forgive. It's all in your hands now, in Jesus' name,
amen!*

Your prayer doesn't need to sound exactly like that, but if
you want to start getting rid of some anxiety and depression, *stop*
ignoring your past pain. Talk to God about it. Take some grievances that you're holding on to (even if you've been holding on for
years) and begin letting go. Start praying about your unforgiveness
daily and watch the level of freedom in your life rise.

## PERMISSION GRANTED

I needed to stop holding on to my unforgiveness. All the pain I
hadn't dealt with was causing me a lot of anxiety and depression.
I needed to face it, feel it, and forgive it.

There's a good chance the same is true for you. Your past pain
has a profound impact on your present life. But it doesn't need to
stay that way—you can heal.

I needed permission to feel the weight of my past.

I needed permission to allow myself to heal from what had
happened.

I needed permission to let go of my desire to make people pay
for what they'd done.

I needed permission to say yes to forgiveness but no to
fellowship.

The more permission my counselors gave me, the easier forgiveness became. And the easier forgiveness became, the more I

began to experience greater levels of peace and joy. And so, let me give you the same permission.

You can stop ignoring the pain in your past. You have permission to face it, feel it, and forgive it! You have permission to say no to fellowship. You have permission to stop holding on to unforgiveness and find the freedom from anxiety and depression you deserve.

# PERFORMING FOR THE CRITICS

Therapists are usually great at circling around issues, but one day during my seven weeks of counseling, one therapist just asked me straight up: "What are the actual things in your life causing you anxiety?"

I really appreciated how blunt the question was and I immediately knew my answer. "Opinions," I told him without skipping a beat. "It's all the people telling me how they think I'm doing at my job."

I'm a pastor, so my life is very public. Especially now that everyone on social media can get ahold of me. Today, everybody with a keyboard and an opinion gets to publicly talk about how they think I'm performing.

Most people are very gracious and encouraging, but once in a while, I'll get a negative review, post, or comment. It's tough for me to brush off criticism, so I expend precious energy worrying about what people have said in the past or may say in the future.

Our church grew fast, which was exciting but also terrifying. The larger our church got, the more opinions I heard. Even when I wasn't getting critiqued, I started getting anxious about the possibility of future criticism coming my way.

I'd go out to the church lobby in between services and hear fifty people say, "Thank you, God has been using this church to change my life." But if I heard one criticism or one critique, I would take it so personally. It would ring loud in my mind. I would play that criticism, critique, post, or comment over and over and over in my mind, and my anxiety and depression would spiral out of control.

As a result, I started performing for people. I began trying to be the person people wanted me to be instead of the person God created me to be. Pretending isn't the only thing we need to stop. We also need to stop performing for the critics.

## PERFORMING VERSUS PERFECTED

I'm going to go out on a limb and guess that I'm not the only one who has ever tried to perform their way out of criticism. You don't have to be a pastor or even a public speaker to know how this feels. Criticism stings. It has the power to flip our emotions upside down and send us into a tailspin. It makes our hearts sink and our minds race, so we do anything we can to avoid it.

And by the way, as bad as other people can be, oftentimes we are our own worst critics. I know people who spend their entire lives trying to please everybody so no one will ever have anything negative to say about them, but then they destroy themselves with their own thinking. They look in the mirror and think things like:

- *I don't like the way I look.*
- *I don't like the way I dress.*
- *I don't like the way I talk.*
- *I don't have a future.*
- *I don't have a purpose.*
- *I don't have hope.*

When I talk about critics, I'm not just talking about other people—I'm also talking about what *you* say about you.

Not even Academy Award–winning actors can perform their way out of criticism. Whether it comes from you or others, it's inevitable. In fact, here's a simple rule of thumb: the greater the influence, the greater the criticism. For some reason (I won't pretend to understand), the more you try to *build people up*, the more critics will try to *tear you down*.

Fortunately, the apostle Paul understood this tension.

We keep coming back to Paul because, as we've talked about a few times, although he was one of the most influential humans ever to live, he was also no stranger to depression (2 Corinthians 1:8).

I know the feeling.

Maybe you do too.

Well, in his letter to his friends in Galatia, we find out one of the causes of that pain was because he was listening to the wrong voices. Paul had plenty of critics, and early on he fell into the trap of giving them too much real estate in his mind. So in the first chapter he said, "Am I now trying to win the approval of human beings, or of God? Or am I trying to please people? If I were still trying to please people, I would not be a servant of Christ" (Galatians 1:10).

According to Paul, we can either spend our time performing for our critics and giving them a certain amount of control over our lives or spend our time serving Christ—but we can't do both. So the only way I can live the kind of life that God has in store for me and walk in the calling God has for my life is to focus on what Christ says instead of the critics.

The best part about serving Christ instead of performing for our critics is that he already made a way for us to be perfect. As the writer of Hebrews said, "For by one sacrifice he has made perfect forever those who are being made holy" (Hebrews 10:14).

Critics say *perform*.

Christ says *perfected*.

We won't ever be able to perform our way out of criticism, but we don't have to. Christ already did that for us by going to the cross to pay the price for our sins!

We are all in the process of "being made holy," and along the way we are going to have good days and bad days. But according to Scripture, Christ already perfected us, which means we get to stop performing!

# CRITICS OR CREATOR?

During my seven weeks of counseling I had to face up to the reality that no matter how well I performed, criticism was going to come. Which meant I needed a new strategy. I had to stop performing for my critics and start finding my value in my Creator.

Did you know that you can actually decide whose voice you are going to listen to?

It took me several weeks of counseling to realize that I didn't have to keep giving so much worth and value to my critics.

When I listened to the critics—my anxiety skyrocketed.

When I listened to my Creator—the result was peace, joy, and confidence.

Peace, joy, and confidence is what every single one of us wants, isn't it? That's why we need to stop performing for our critics and begin listening to our Creator.

In part 2, I told you about my war chest—twenty promises from Scripture that I make a habit of proclaiming aloud when I need to start choosing to remember who God is and who he says I am. Now I want to share with you my five go-to verses for when I need to stop performing for critics. These are five truths my Creator says about me. Whenever critics start to talk, I immediately turn back to my Creator.

I challenge you to do the same thing. Put these verses up on your mirror, make them the screen saver on your phone, or save them as a file on your computer. Every time a critic tries to talk about you, combat the negativity by reminding yourself what your Creator says about you!

By the way, these five are my arsenal. As always, your weapons of choice may be a little different. You can customize this with whatever verses work for you, but these are the ones that work for me.

So many mental health problems have been caused by constantly ruminating over the comments of critical people, so let these verses begin to settle your anxiety and lift you out of the pit of depression.

### Verse #1: Psalm 139:13-14

> For you created my inmost being;
>> you knit me together in my mother's womb.
> I praise you because I am fearfully and
>> wonderfully made;
>> your works are wonderful,
> I know that full well.

You may have surprised your parents, but you didn't surprise God. He knit you together perfectly and on purpose.

### Verse #2: Ephesians 2:10

> "For we are God's handiwork, created in Christ Jesus to do good works, which God prepared in advance for us to do."

You aren't just okay; you are a masterpiece! When God made you, he called everyone over to say, "You've got to see this! Look at my boy. Look at my girl. That right there is a masterpiece!"

### Verse #3: John 15:16

> "You did not choose me, but I chose you and appointed you so that you might go and bear fruit—fruit that will last—and so that whatever you ask in my name the Father will give you."

When I feel overwhelmed by my responsibilities in life and struggle with not feeling like I am enough, I remind myself that I didn't choose myself for this purpose—*God chose me!*

Yes, I can raise this child.

Yes, I can lead this organization.

Yes, I can survive this tragedy.

Yes, I can walk in my calling.

Because the Creator of the universe chose me!

### Verse #4: 1 Thessalonians 5:24

"The one who calls you is faithful, and he will do it."

Not only did God call me, but he also does the heavy lifting for me. It's okay that I feel in over my head today. I'm going to give my anxiety permission to take a rest. Today, I'm going to worry less about whatever I'm going through. God's got it under control, and he will take care of it!

### Verse #5: Romans 11:29

"For God's gifts and his call are irrevocable."

No matter how many times I've messed up, God's still got me. Even when my own critical voice in my head tries to say, *God has to be done with you by now!* I remind myself that he still loves me. He's still with me. And he has a calling for me because the plans God has for me have not expired or been revoked. They are irrevocable.

# THE MAN IN THE ARENA

Dealing with critics is not a new phenomenon; people have been wrestling with this topic for thousands of years. As we just saw, writers of Scripture have plenty of wisdom to share with us from their experiences, but there are lots of others too. One of my favorite quotes about dealing with the critics in our lives comes from Theodore Roosevelt. At the time, he was speaking to a large crowd about this very topic of not letting the critical voices affect your life.

It's worth reading the whole thing, so let's look together at his words:

It is not the critic who counts; not the man who points out how the strong man stumbles, or where the doer of deeds could have done them better. The credit belongs to the man who is actually in the arena, whose face is marred by dust and sweat and blood; who strives valiantly; who errs, who comes short again and again, because there is no effort without error and shortcoming; but who does actually strive to do the deeds; who knows great enthusiasms, the great devotions; who spends himself in a worthy cause; who at the best knows in the end the triumph of high achievement, and who at the worst, if he fails, at least fails while daring greatly, so that his place shall never be with those cold and timid souls who neither know victory nor defeat.[6]

And the crowd went wild—as they should have!

It's easier to critique than it is to create. So there will always be critics sitting up in the grandstands, lobbing their opinions at you. But at the end of the day, what really matters is that we stay in the fight. And even when we experience a few defeats, we get back up and continue daring greatly.

You get to choose which voices you listen to. If you want to battle anxiety and depression at another level today, decide to start listening less to the critics and more to your Creator and embrace the peace, joy, and confidence that accompanies that decision.

You'll never make everyone happy. So stop trying to. Stop

performing. Criticism is inevitable, but it is not the end of the world. You just have to remind yourself which voice you are going to listen to. Refuse to allow the critical voices in your mind to cause you anxiety and depression.

Today, you can decide to focus on the Word of God.

Today, you can decide to focus on the truth that you were created on purpose, with a purpose. You are a masterpiece. You are called. You are chosen. So walk in the plans that God has for you!

Stop letting critical voices take you away from your calling, joy, or peace.

You can choose to stop performing for the critics. You can choose to stop listening to the critical voices giving you anxiety and depression. And you can choose to say yes to walking in confidence.

# COMPARING YOUR CALLING

There is one last thing we all need to stop doing on our journey to freedom from anxiety and depression. I'm telling you, this last one is huge. It's a trap we all fall into in our own ways. And most of us don't even realize it. The good news is, once we recognize we are doing it and we get intentional about shutting it down, we have a fighting chance at finding freedom.

I'm talking about comparison.

And if you are wondering what comparison has to do with anxiety and depression, the answer is *everything*. At least for me. There aren't many things in this world that pour gasoline on the anxiety and depression fire in my soul faster than comparison.

Comparison leaves me feeling insecure.

Not enough.

Insignificant.

Void of purpose.

All the things that make me spiral down into the depths of depression. To share another quote commonly attributed to Theodore Roosevelt, "Comparison is the thief of joy."

How spot-on is that?

And Roosevelt lived before social media—before we all had the ability to compare ourselves to the entire world in our pockets.

I'm not trying to be the anti–social media guy. I do, though, want to warn all of us who use it, or have loved ones who do, to be cautious. The next time you spend some time scrolling, take inventory of two things:

1. The types of posts you see
2. The way it makes you feel

I can almost guarantee what the answer is going to be to both of those. The answer to the first question is, you are going to see everyone's highlight reel. Very few people ever decide to post the low points of their lives. Which means, if you are anything like me, the answer to the second question is, it'll make you feel like you aren't enough. Here are the thoughts that run through my head: *Wow, I don't have that great of a car, house, family, or vacation. I guess I'm not that great of a parent. Or friend. Or employee. Or leader. I guess I don't really do anything all that important. I guess I don't have a purpose like they do.*

*I don't travel like she does.*

*I don't earn an income like him.*

*I don't walk and talk like they do.*

*Maybe I'm just less than.*

It's almost impossible to spend a significant amount of time on social media and not feel more insecure and unstable. I mean, have you ever spent twenty minutes looking at social media and felt better about your life? Probably not often.

Why?

Because social media has turned into one big comparison game. And since our *normal* can't compete with other people's highlight reels, it leaves all of us feeling sad. And for a lot of us, it ultimately leads straight to depression. Comparison ruins us. Or, as the Proverb puts it, "Envy rots the bones" (14:30). And when we struggle with anxiety and depression, scrolling just pours gasoline on a fire that already felt impossible to put out.

If we want to experience freedom from anxiety and depression, we need to *stop* comparing.

In his letter to Ephesus, Paul implored his friends to stop comparing their lives to others' and instead begin valuing, appreciating, and being grateful for who they themselves were. "For we are His workmanship, created in Christ Jesus for good works, which God prepared beforehand so that we would walk in them" (Ephesians 2:10 NASB). We are God's workmanship! But every time we scroll, we fall into the comparison trap; we forget God crafted us and feel more like we can't measure up.

Let's get practical and talk about some tangible ways we can all stop falling into the comparison trap so that we can become the men and women God created us to be.

## STOP SCROLLING BEFORE BED

One of the practical takeaways from my seven weeks of counseling was how important high-quality sleep is for mental health. My problem was, I wasn't getting any. My counselors introduced me to a term called "sleep hygiene."

Then they politely told me that mine sucked.

My sleep wasn't clean.

And one of the main reasons was because I was staring at screens all night while I tried to fall asleep. I'd lay in bed, scroll, and end my day feeling like I didn't accomplish as much as everyone else.

But it gets worse.

Apparently, screen lights mimic the light our eyes take in during the middle of the day. So they explained that all my screen usage before bedtime was actually tricking my body into thinking it was daytime, causing my body to fight against my desire for sleep.

In other words, I was setting myself up for failure.

They challenged me to be completely off screens for one hour before bedtime, and if I couldn't fall asleep, my option was to read. Nothing work related. Nothing about how to be a better leader or anything that would cause my brain to engage in critical thinking. They told me to just read a novel or something for fun. And if I really couldn't fall asleep, they told me to pick up my Bible and read through the book of Leviticus. (*Lord, forgive them. I'm not the one saying that book moves slow; it was my counselors, and I'm as mad at them as you are right now!*)

Sleep matters. It helps us battle anxiety and depression in big ways. I'm going to be honest; I hate this rule. But I hate being caught in anxiety and depression even more. We need to clean up our sleep, and the first way to do it is to put down the screens and stop scrolling an hour before bedtime.

# REMEMBER YOUR CALLING

I can't tell you how many days and nights I've lost joy and had to deal with depression because I spent time on social media comparing every aspect of my life to everyone else's highlight reel—not their real life. Nobody shares that. I was seeing their highlight reels. And yet, I compared my real life and low points to their high points. That is a recipe for depression. I have fallen victim to it more times than I care to admit. And the worst part is, those people and their calling have nothing to do with me and mine. There is a reason God has placed me on this earth. My job is to remember what Paul said to the church in Ephesus. I am God's workmanship, and I am here for a reason.

The same is true for you.

The next thing we need to do is remember our calling because the more we focus on our calling, the less we feel the need to compare. The reason we get so caught up in other people's highlight reels is because we forget why God has us on this earth. You are here for a reason. You are uniquely wired. You are created on purpose and for a purpose.

Your job is not to keep up with everyone else. Your job is to be who you are and do what you are here to do.

I'm not saying you have to deactivate all your social media accounts. I'm just saying please be aware of the comparison trap and begin paying attention to what happens in your soul when you start to scroll. And before you jump on, take five seconds to remind yourself what God says about you. You are God's workmanship. Never forget it.

These days when I feel myself going down that road, I have a line that I repeat back to myself. There are days where I have to whisper this line to myself an embarrassing number of times, but I'm telling you, it's powerful. When I feel my mental health beginning to unravel because I'm comparing myself to others, I stop and think, *I can celebrate their calling, but I will walk in mine.*

This is so important that I'm going to say it again. Whenever you feel comparison starting to creep into your life—whether it's through social media or just living life and observing others do the same—one of the best ways to stop playing the game is to constantly remind yourself: *I can celebrate their calling, but I will walk in mine.*

Try it!

Every time you go to school and see someone else who is smarter, cooler, or better at sports than you, remind yourself—*I can celebrate their calling, but I will walk in mine.*

Every time you go to the office and talk to your coworker who gets more praise and promotions than you, remind yourself—*I can celebrate their calling, but I will walk in mine.*

Every time you pull into the neighborhood and see a house that is bigger or better kept than yours or a family that doesn't seem to have any problems, remind yourself—*I can celebrate their calling, but I will walk in mine.*

Every time you go to that family function and start to feel like everyone else is living out their dreams, but you can't seem to get it together, remind yourself—*I can celebrate their calling, but I will walk in mine.*

And every time you jump on social media and see that person in your field who appears to do your job way better than you, remind yourself—*I can celebrate their calling, but I will walk in mine.*

That's where the confidence is.

That's where the peace is.

That's where the joy is.

And when I'm feeling those three things, it's difficult to be depressed and anxious.

## GUARD YOUR HEART

God's Word says, "Above all else, guard your heart" (Proverbs 4:23). Is that what you are doing? Take an honest look at your social media intake. As you go through your day, pay attention to how you watch other people and be honest with yourself about how it affects your life. Ask yourself, *Is this good for me? Am I spending more time looking over the fence at everyone else's life than simply valuing, appreciating, and celebrating mine?*

Remember, you can celebrate their calling, but you have to walk in yours.

Have you been playing the comparison game? Have you been allowing jealousy and envy to rot your bones? If so, what are you willing to do to turn this around?

Are you willing to unfollow some people (even good people) if watching them on social media makes you feel more depressed?

Are you willing to take a little time off? Why not do a twenty-one-day detox from all social media and use that time to reassess some boundaries for your life?

I still use social media, but way less than I used to. In fact, at one point, I took a few months completely off. My soul felt so healthy, and my confidence began to rise. You'll know what's best for you. But above all else, "guard your heart" (Proverbs 4:23).

Remember, comparison is the thief of joy. But when we walk

in the plans and purpose God has for us, we don't have time to compare—we are too busy creating our own lives. That's what fuels our souls and ushers in peace, joy, confidence, and freedom. Get in the habit of guarding your heart because the only way to experience joy is to stop trying to walk in the plans and purposes God has for somebody else.

## A WEDDING IN THE SNOW

All of this sounds great on paper, but a while back, I learned this lesson firsthand. It started when I had to call a friend of mine to come over and help me fix my garbage disposal. After he finished, I asked if I could pay him, but he refused.

"Please," I said. "I don't want to take advantage of you. Let me pay you."

But he kept refusing. We hashed it out for a few minutes, but then he finally pointed at his employee who was standing next to him, a young guy (who we'll call Brian), and said, "If you want to pay me, perform his wedding ceremony."

I don't do many weddings these days because of my schedule. But I couldn't really say no at that point, could I?

Every now and then, there will be a special occasion, and of course, I am honored to do it. I wanted to honor my friend who helps me out a lot, and so I immediately said, "Yes, I will perform Brian's wedding."

A few weeks later, I met with Brian and his fiancée (let's call her Kelly). They came up to my office, and we sat down to plan their wedding, which I soon realized would be the smallest wedding ceremony I had ever been a part of. Kelly said she would not have anyone from her family at the wedding (which made me wonder what her story was), and Brian informed me that only his parents, a sibling or two, and a photographer would be there from his side.

So we were talking about a party of about six or seven people. They also informed me that it would be an outdoor ceremony in the mountains, west of where we live in Denver. And that the wedding was still a few months away.

At that point in my life, I was really struggling with the comparison game. I was on social media looking at other pastors who seemed to be invited to speak at bigger conferences than me. Who got to hang out with famous and influential people. Who had way more followers on social media than I did. Who dressed better, spoke better, and went on better vacations.

Or so it appeared on my phone.

Their lives just seemed to be more important than mine. You get it. Regardless of what you do for a living, I'm sure some people appear to be doing it better.

I was in the middle of the comparison game and feeling very insecure about myself when I received a text message inviting me to a private event with some of the most influential and well-known pastors in our country. We were going to spend a night in one of their homes, just talking about all the things we had been learning. Then the next day, we were going to ride a bus together to the University of Alabama, sit in the locker room, and listen to a leadership talk from Nick Saban, arguably one of the greatest leaders and football coaches of all time.

I couldn't believe it.

Why were they inviting me?

How was I a part of this?

It didn't matter. I was. I got the text. I felt like I had arrived. Like maybe my life did matter. Maybe I had some purpose. I could already see the social media posts and pictures of all of us influential pastors together. I was going to be in the club! *God must really like me now.* I got my plane tickets, hotel reservations, rented a car, and the only thing left to do was go hang out with these guys I was so envious of.

And then I received a tragic phone call.

"Shawn," I could hear the tone in my assistant's voice, and I knew this wasn't going to be good. "I don't know how we missed this. You are supposed to be in Alabama on Tuesday and Wednesday."

"Yeah, I know, I can't wait," I blurted out, feeling like a *but* was inevitable.

"Shawn, remember that wedding you agreed to months ago? It's on Tuesday."

My heart sank.

*This can't be happening. Am I going to miss the opportunity of a lifetime for a six-person wedding? There can't be a God in heaven.*

I told some pastor friends what had happened, and all of them said the same exact thing: "This is a once-in-a-lifetime opportunity. Call the couple you barely know, explain what happened, promise to get another person on staff to perform the wedding, and get to Alabama."

I thought long and hard about their advice—trust me. But something in my soul just wouldn't let me do it. I knew I needed to go through with the wedding.

But then the plot thickened.

I got another call from my assistant, who informed me that there was supposed to be a blizzard on Tuesday evening.

Remember, this wedding was outside, in the mountains. "What if you cancel your trip to Alabama and then the wedding gets canceled?"

So I called Brian. I explained to him that I had made a mistake and double-booked myself, but I was 100 percent still going to do the wedding. I just wanted to make sure that they wouldn't cancel it and move it to another date since the weather would be pretty bad. Brian was unbelievably gracious. He told me not to worry about it at all; he knew how busy I was and said that they could find someone else to do the wedding. But then he told me that regardless of how bad the weather got, they were going to do the wedding that day.

I just knew in my heart that the right thing was to do this wedding, so I told Brian I would meet him on the side of the mountain next Tuesday.

I drove up to the mountains with my suit on, feeling completely sorry for myself and picturing the laughter, the fun, and the social media posts that I was missing out on with all those really important (and, in my mind, "famous") pastors in Alabama.

When I finally got to the mountain, I discovered a dirt parking lot, which meant that it was mostly mud because of the snow. My first step out of the car was into a puddle of mud that ruined my new dress shoes. (That may sound dramatic, but I love shoes; don't judge me.)

From there, I walked down this long dirt path to this area on the side of the mountain, and I performed a wedding ceremony while snow began to fall. The ceremony lasted about fifteen minutes tops. Then the couple and the photographer stayed, and I began to walk back to my car.

As I went, Brian's dad met me on the path.

"Listen, Shawn, the kids don't have a lot of money," he said. "I don't know if they were able to pay you for doing this or not. Let me make this right."

"Absolutely not," I said. "It's my honor to be here, and it's my honor to do this wedding. Congratulations."

"Well, I just wanted to say thank you, it's really special for them to have you here, you know, because of Kelly's story and all."

"Wait, what?" I said. "I'm sorry, I don't know her story."

And so he went into it, and I couldn't believe what I was hearing.

When she was four or five, Kelly's father shot himself and died by suicide. Then one day, when she was seventeen, Kelly went home and saw her brother (who struggled with mental illness) shoot and kill her mother. He then began chasing Kelly and her sister around the house, trying to kill them. Her sister jumped out of a two-story window to escape. She fell to the ground, broke her back, and now has paraplegia. Kelly locked herself in her bedroom, and her brother began shooting at the door, trying to get in to kill her. But the cops finally showed up, and when he realized they were there, he shot himself and died.

"She has nobody," he said. "Her mom is dead. Her dad is dead. Her brother's dead." I was shaking as I stood on the side of the mountain, and it wasn't because of the snow.

He went on to explain that she became an atheist. She gave up on God and began to believe that there was no way there could be a good God in heaven if something like that happened. And she would wake up with night terrors almost every night.

Then somebody brought her to Red Rocks Church one weekend when I happened to be speaking, and God did something profound and amazing in her life. He brought healing to some deep wounds in her soul, and she gave her life fully over to God.

He looked right at me and said, "And she had a dream in her heart that someday she would meet the right man and that you, Pastor Shawn, would perform her wedding."

My legs almost gave out from under me as he turned to rejoin the celebration. My face was flushed, and tears were rolling down my cheeks.

"By the way," he said, turning back to face me one last time. "You are probably wondering why we did the wedding on a Tuesday in weather like this. We did the wedding today because today's her mom's birthday."

"I . . . I . . . had no idea. I'm absolutely honored to be here," I said. He thanked me, and then I went and sat in my car and just wept. I was crying uncontrollably. And then I just started immediately repenting.

*God, I'm so sorry. I wanted so badly to be like everybody else—to be like the people I've been comparing myself to—that I almost missed out on this moment. I almost missed out on one of the most purpose-filled moments I've ever experienced in my entire life so I could hang out with what, in my mind, were famous pastors.*

Here's what I learned that day on the side of that mountain. I wanted to be like all those well-known pastors, the ones with a bazillion followers on social media. But not one of them could have performed that wedding for that couple the way that I could. I was the only person who could walk in my calling that day.

I can't describe to you how amazing it felt to stop comparing my calling with everyone else. I suddenly felt a deep peace. I was flooded with joy, with confidence, and with freedom.

Freedom from comparison.

Freedom from anxiety.

Freedom from insecurity.

Freedom from depression.

Purpose was defining my life, and it felt so good. God reminded me that day to stop looking over the fence at everyone else's life. I can celebrate your calling, but I'm going to walk in mine because that's where the purpose is.

And I'm telling you, the same thing is true for you today. Other people may appear to have it more together than you. They may have more followers. They may appear to be living the life you want to live. But they can't walk in your calling. That is reserved for you. And the day you start to believe that, anxiety and depression will flee. I challenge you right now to begin to embrace yourself exactly the way God made you and exactly where God has you. Begin to walk in your calling today with confidence because only you can be you today!

Don't let comparison rob you of your calling.

## STOP TO START

- *Stop* pretending.
- *Stop* holding on to unforgiveness.
- *Stop* performing.
- *Stop* comparing.

While I believe every single one of us will have to deal with and learn to put a stop to the four things listed above, don't forget that anxiety and depression are slightly different for all of us. So remember the two questions I asked you to focus on earlier:

1. Are there things in my life that I do consistently that cause my anxiety to go up?
2. Are there things that are in my control that cause me to spiral into a state of depression?

This is the time for you to really think about these two questions. I just shared with you the four answers I came up with, but what's most important is for you to answer these two questions for yourself. Ask those closest to you to tell you what they think your blind spots might be. Spend some time in prayer asking God to reveal to you the areas in your life that need to come to a stop. Remember God loves you too much to let you keep going the way you are now, so let's spend some time coming up with real answers. Once you have those answers, you can begin taking practical steps toward stopping the things in your life that are elevating your anxiety and depression. It'll change the game!

———

This section was not easy, but you made it through. Congratulations! Hopefully by now you realize my goal is not to be a killjoy. I'm not here to stop you from having any fun, just to stop you from continuing down paths that are destroying your mental health. The goal is not just to *stop* unhealthy things but also to free you up to *start* filling that space with healthy things!

Jesus said it best: "The thief comes only to steal and kill and destroy; I have come that they may have life, and have it to the full" (John 10:10). When we stop doing all the things that steal, kill, and destroy our lives, like pretending, performing, and comparing, we have way more space, energy, and capacity to start living the abundant life God has for us.

Sometimes in order to start we first have to stop.

When you are willing to do that, I'm telling you, anxiety and depression will start to lose their grip on your life, and you will begin walking in joy and confidence. And anytime you see someone who appears to be doing better than you, you'll cheer them on and remind yourself—*I can celebrate their calling, but I will walk in mine.*

# Part 4
# *REMEMBER*

# GOD IS WITH YOU

We've covered an awful lot of ground so far in this book. By now, I'm sure you've realized just how real this fight for your freedom is. If you've been applying these principles, you've probably had some victorious moments, where it's felt like you've taken ground and made serious moves in your battle against anxiety and depression.

But along the way, you've probably also had some not-so-great moments. As any fighter will tell you, you're never going to leave the ring without taking a few hits. This is a book about taking the fight to the Enemy. The problem is, the Enemy fights back. Some days may feel amazing and full of hope, like you are taking a step forward. But other days, it may feel like you are taking two steps back.

The good news is, even when you feel like you are losing some battles, we know that God's already won the war. So the final step in your fight for freedom from anxiety and depression is to talk about the three things you need to remember when it feels like this whole thing isn't working for you. The Enemy loves to get in our heads and convince us we are losing ground, but when we can remember these truths, we can easily spot and expose the lies.

Here are the three truths you need to remember:

1. God is with you.
2. God is working.
3. God has a plan.

When you can get these three statements not just in your head but also in your heart, you'll head back into the battlefield with so much confidence it'll shock you!

### Truth #1: God Is with You

We've been talking a lot about a guy named Joshua. Remember, he was the one who built the memorial we read about in chapter 8 and marched around Jericho until the walls fell like we discussed in chapter 6. But Joshua had to overcome many obstacles before the Israelites even got to Jericho. For this final section, I want to take a closer look at the events that led up to that victorious day in Jericho. As it turns out, God was at work the whole time. God was teaching Joshua how to remember the past so that he could be victorious in the present.

And I believe God wants to do the same for you.

To fully grasp the story of Joshua, we need to start with another man. His mentor. A man named Moses. Moses was a murderer on the run who God ended up using to free the entire nation of Israel from roughly four hundred years of slavery in Egypt. It's an incredible story, but it was followed by forty years of wandering in the wilderness on the way to the promised land.

They got stuck.

And Moses never made it into the promised land. He got them right up to the border, and then he passed away. Here's what Scripture says about how those close to Moses were feeling when he died: "The Israelites grieved for Moses in the plains of Moab thirty days, until the time of weeping and mourning was over" (Deuteronomy 34:8).

Does anyone resonate with those words?

Talk about some great words to describe how we feel when we're depressed. Our souls feel heavy, and we find ourselves grieving, mourning, and when it's real bad, even weeping. And if you are anything like the Israelites, it usually doesn't get better after one afternoon—they grieved for thirty whole days.

You really can't blame them either. Remember, these guys had been through an awful lot. Four hundred years of slavery, forty years of wandering, and then, before they even made it into the promised land, their leader passed away. It's no wonder they spiraled into an entire month of grieving.

That's where we meet a man named Joshua.

Joshua was Moses' right-hand man. His ride or die. His mentee. Which means, as you can imagine, Joshua probably had the hardest time with his friend's death. Out of everyone weeping and grieving for thirty days, there's a good chance he was weeping and mourning the most. That's where we pick up the story of Joshua—after a season of mourning and crying for a month straight.

We know that feeling, don't we?

When your soul feels so heavy that you don't want to get out of bed in the morning, when your heart aches, your stomach hurts, you feel lethargic, and you wonder if the pain will ever end.

Those days where everything feels wrong.

We feel wrong about our sadness.

We feel wrong about our depression.

And then, to top it off, we feel wrong about even feeling wrong.

Joshua felt all of that in the plains of Moab for thirty days. Remember, don't make the mistake of thinking these heroes from the Bible had it all together or never had any seasons of sadness.

They were humans—just like you and me.

However, when Joshua was at his lowest point, God came to him with a message. This message is going to blow you away. And before you read it, please hear me: no matter how you are feeling right now, God is saying the same thing to you today. Even if you are at your absolute lowest point, let the God of the universe speak these words to you: "Have I not commanded you? Be strong and courageous. Do not be afraid; do not be discouraged, for the LORD your God will be with you wherever you go" (Joshua 1:9).

God knew how bad things were. He knew how overwhelmed Joshua felt. He knew how hard it must have been for Joshua to lose his best friend/mentor and then immediately step up and fill his shoes. So when God told Joshua to be strong and courageous, notice the source of the strength. God reminded Joshua that he was going with him. God would be with him every step of the way. Joshua's courage wasn't supposed to come from his own strength—it was meant to come from God's strength.

God had a purpose for him, even though Joshua couldn't fathom what that purpose was in the moment. God implored him to get up, dust himself off, and be strong and courageous.

You need to know the same thing right now, especially in

the moments when you feel like you are losing ground. No matter how you feel today, you can be strong and courageous because God is going with you.

You don't need to know what is going to happen next.

You don't need a full rundown of the plans.

All you need to know is God is with you! He's right by your side. He'll be with you all day and all night, and when you wake up tomorrow, he'll still be right there. It doesn't matter how bad it gets—God's not going anywhere.

Can you let God speak to you right now?

No matter how bad your anxiety or depression is, the God of the universe is saying: *I am with you!*

When we know our all-powerful Father is with us and has our backs, it changes everything.

It changes the way we walk.

It changes the way we talk.

It changes the way we feel.

It changes the way we act.

When we remember God is going with us, it changes the entire game.

## WHO'S GOT YOUR BACK?

When I was eight years old, my family and I lived out in the country, so I rode the bus to and from school every day. When I was in third grade, our bus driver gave us assigned seats, forcing me to sit next to a teenage boy who was twice my size.

We'll call him Justin.

For whatever reason, Justin liked to pick on me. Even though there was a giant age difference, he'd call me names, punch me in the arm, and take up the whole seat so that I was barely able to balance on the very edge of the row. Even as I write this all these years later, I'd love to invite Justin to three five-minute rounds in an octagon (but that's beside the point).

One day I came home from school with a folder full of papers from the last several weeks. They were all graded and marked up with comments, and I was supposed to show them to my parents.

As soon as I sat down on the edge of the row, Justin grabbed the folder from me. I tried to get it back, but with his size advantage, he kept me back with ease. Then he grabbed a Sharpie out of his bag and began to write cuss words all over my assignments. The words filled the entire page, all the way from the top to the bottom. And I'm talking about the really bad words, like the one that starts with f.

Remember, I was only eight.

I didn't know what to do, what to say, or how to stand up for myself. Instead, I just sat back and watched it all happen, thinking about how strange this situation was. When I got home and my parents asked me for the folder, I tried to hide it. But when you are eight, you aren't nearly as clever as you think you are, so my parents quickly figured out where it was.

"What happened here?" asked my dad. (For clarity, my "dad" married my mom and adopted me.)

His voice was stern and had one of those tones that let me know I better have a good explanation. I didn't know what to say, so I just told him that Justin, the high school boy who lived down the street, had done it.

He kept staring at the papers for what felt like forever. "Get in the car," he said, finally breaking the silence.

"What?" I asked, trying to figure out what was going to happen next.

"I said get in the car, now."

We jumped in the car and sat in silence. I was terrified; my dad was not the type of man you wanted to make angry. He was also not the type of guy who liked to waste gas, so instead of cranking the air conditioner, he rolled the windows down, and we drove to Justin's house.

When we got there, he left the windows in his car down, so I could hear everything happening on the front porch as clear as day. He walked up and started pounding on the front door. It wasn't one of those friendly "Hey neighbor, I'd love to meet you" kind of knocks. It was more like an "I'm here to do some damage" sort of knock.

Eventually, Justin's dad came to the door, and unfortunately for him, he was a much smaller man than my dad. My dad did not introduce himself or attempt to make any sort of small talk. He didn't open with, "Hey, there might be a little issue at school we should address."

None of that.

Instead, he held up a stack of papers with the f-word written across the front and said, "You see this?" Keep in mind, this was Kansas. Out in the country, we just played by different rules.

Justin's dad looked so confused. "Um, yes?" he said timidly.

Then my dad threw the stack of papers in his face and the pages fluttered to the ground. He took another step forward and got in Justin's dad's face. "If your kid ever touches my son again," he yelled, "I'll be back. And I'm not going to touch your boy, but I will deal with you. We clear?"

"Ye-ye-yes sir, we're clear," Justin's dad said with the smallest, most fearful voice I've ever heard from an adult man. Then my dad slammed the door shut, slammed their screen door shut (just for effect), and walked back to the car. Before he even got back, I could already hear Justin's dad yelling for his son and the sound of discipline beginning in the house.

For better or worse, my dad took care of the problem.

You should've seen me get on that bus the next day. I walked back to my seat with my shoulders back and my head held high. I had a brand-new swagger. Justin was already there, and I sat right down, looked him in the eyes, and said, "What's up, Justin?"

He didn't utter a word. Instead, he scooted over as far as he could to give me as much room as possible, and he stared out the window.

I walked different.

I talked different.

I acted different.

Why? Because I knew my dad had my back.

I believe the same thing will start to happen to you when you realize that your heavenly Father is with you. When you know that the Creator of the universe has your back, you will begin to put your shoulders back and walk with a whole new swagger.

I know anxiety is real.

I know depression is real.

I know how scary it feels in the middle of the storm.

But you need to hear the same thing Joshua needed to hear all those years ago. The God of the universe—the one who speaks and creates oceans and mountain ranges, the God who does the impossible and isn't afraid of anything or anyone—is walking with you.

He is with you.

He is in your corner.

He has got your back.

He is fighting for you.

That ought to change the way you think about yourself today. That ought to change the way you talk, the way you walk, the way you act. The God of the universe is on your side!

Anxiety and depression may have picked on you your entire life. But once you know your heavenly Father has your back, suddenly this battle becomes a battle you can win. Not because you're strong enough but because your God is.

And he's right there with you.

You have to remember:

*Truth #1: **God is with you**—even if you can't feel it.*

# GOD IS WORKING

The second truth you need to remember and get in the habit of preaching to yourself when you feel like you are losing ground is that God hasn't stopped working in your life. In our lower moments, it certainly feels like he has, doesn't it?

Scripture reminds us, "And we know that in all things God works for the good of those who love him, who have been called according to his purpose" (Romans 8:28).

Did you catch that? The Bible says that God is working *all things* together for good. I know that's hard to believe, especially in the middle of all your anxiety and depression. When your emotions are all over the place, it feels impossible that God is at work. But *all things* means *all things*.

In the middle of your worst day of anxiety—God is at work.

In the middle of your worst state of depression—God is at work.

In the middle of your deepest state of hopelessness—God is at work.

When it feels like everything around you is falling apart, like every situation around you is going in the wrong direction, and everything that should be right feels wrong, remember—God is at work in your life.

Not because you can see it.

Not because you can feel it.

Not because you understand it.

But because God's Word declares it. And God's Word trumps your feelings every single day. I'm telling you, no matter how you feel, *remember*: God is at work in your life right now!

## STAND IN THE RIVER

Joshua had to learn this lesson through experience.

Remember where we left off in his story. His best friend and mentor had just passed away, and he got charged with the task of leading the Israelites into the promised land. That meant his job was to do what Moses couldn't do, which may sound good on paper but presented a whole lot of challenges. The first problem was that the Jordan River was standing in between the nation of Israel and the promised land. And we aren't just talking about a little creek you'd step over on a hike—this was a massive river that the Bible tells us was at flood stage.

In other words, this was an impossible task.

Joshua was depressed over the loss of his leader, and I'd imagine his anxiety was at an all-time high because of the task facing him. But God said to Joshua, "Do not be afraid; do not be discouraged, for the LORD your God will be with you wherever you go" (Joshua 1:9).

The first thing Joshua needed to remember when he had his back against the wall was that God was going with him. But then the second truth he needed to remember was that God was at work in his life, even when Joshua couldn't see it.

Joshua was about to try to do the impossible—take the nation of Israel across the Jordan River in flood season. That was a suicide mission; no doubt many who tried it would drown. But those were his marching orders from God, so he was committed to moving forward.

Check out what happened next:

> Now the Jordan is at flood stage all during harvest. Yet as soon as the priests who carried the ark reached the Jordan and their feet touched the water's edge, the water from upstream stopped flowing. It piled up in a heap a great distance away, at a town called Adam in the vicinity of Zarethan, while the water flowing down to the Sea of the Arabah (that is, the Dead Sea) was completely cut off. So the people crossed over opposite Jericho. (Joshua 3:15–16)

If you read that too fast (or if you grew up in church and have heard that story one too many times), you may have just missed the real drama. Do you remember how God brought the Israelites out of slavery in Egypt forty years earlier?

He did it by parting the Red Sea just long enough for them to cross it on dry ground and escape the Egyptian army.

That must've been the greatest miracle they had ever experienced. You can't see something like that and not keep talking about it. Which means, for the last forty years, the Israelites had been wandering in the wilderness talking about that miracle.

This new generation of Israelites probably heard that story a thousand times. They grew up hearing their parents tell it over and over again at the dinner table.

"We just walked right up to the water, and God did the rest—I've never seen anything like it."

"It was an instant miracle. The second we took a step forward, God parted the sea right in front of our eyes. We stepped—it parted. Just like that!"

And now, this next generation was faced with a similar situation. There was a massive river standing between them and the place they wanted to be, and God told them to do the same thing—even though it looked impossible, their job was to walk toward the water.

If you read that passage too fast, you may have just figured this miracle was a cheap knockoff of the first, but that's actually not what happened. Let's slow down a bit and take a closer look at this passage because I want to show you what really happened.

> Now the Jordan is at flood stage all during harvest. Yet as soon as the priests who carried the ark reached the Jordan and their feet touched the water's edge, the water from upstream stopped flowing. It piled up in a heap a great distance away, at a town called Adam. (3:15–16)

Did you spot the difference?

If you haven't brushed up on your ancient Israel geography in a while, you may have missed it, but I'm telling you, this is good. Try to take it in.

When the Israelites stepped into the river, a miracle immediately took place. The water piled up and stopped running. But it didn't happen right where the Israelites were standing (like it did for their parents forty years ago at the Red Sea); it happened in a town called Adam, which was "a great distance away" (Joshua 3:16).

Why is that so important? Think about it—what happens when a river is cut off that far upstream?

And no, this isn't a trick question.

The answer is *nothing*.

At least at first.

If the water was cut off far upstream, that means there was still many miles' worth of running water that had to pass the Israelites before they witnessed their miracle. The miracle happened immediately, but depending on how fast the river was flowing, the Israelites wouldn't have seen it for what could have been hours.

Think about that for a second.

They had to stand in the river feeling ridiculous, confused, embarrassed, and probably really anxious for several hours. What would have been going through your mind if you'd been in their position? I'd probably have started feeling like God had forgotten about me.

But nothing could have been further from the truth.

God was on the move. A miracle was taking place. He was working in their lives in such a powerful way that it was about to change their lives forever. But they couldn't see it.

When they took a step of faith, the miracle happened. But in order to see that miracle take place, they had to stand in the tension for several hours and wait on God.

It is so important that we understand and remember this principle. Faith put the miracle in motion but standing on God's promise brought the miracle to fruition. In the darker moments, from our limited perspective, it can start to feel like God has for-gotten about us. But even when we can't see it, God is working!

# IT'S SORTA LIKE PIZZA

We just took a deep dive into this Old Testament story. I don't know about you, but I get confused easily and sometimes I need things explained to me like I'm a third grader. In case you got lost amid all those names of cities and rivers, let's simplify this concept with an analogy.

Just order a pizza tonight.

I'm serious. That's all you have to do to understand the com-plexity of this story. Order a pizza and tell yourself that pizza is a miracle (because let's be honest, if you order it from the right spot, it will be).

The second you make that phone call and ask for that miracu-lous pizza to come into your life, a whole team of people will get to work.

Years ago, I worked at a Pizza Hut, so I've seen this process happen hundreds of times. We'd get the order, grab some dough, and get to work. Over the next few minutes, we'd smother the pizza with just the right ratio of sauce and cheese. After that, we'd add on the toppings, cover it with even more cheese, and place it in the oven. When enough time had passed, we'd take it out of the oven, cut it, put it in a box, and hand it off to the delivery guy. Then they'd throw it in their car, put one of those super official signs on their roof, and speed off to your house.

What does all of that have to do with the story of Joshua in the Jordan River?

Get this—since we've already established that pizza is a miracle, it's fair to say that the miracle happened the moment you made the phone call. However, the pizza didn't show up at your doorstep for forty-five minutes. You couldn't see it, but there was a process of that pizza becoming a reality in your life.

If you didn't know how the process of ordering a pizza worked, you may have lost hope the moment you hung up the phone and realized you were still hungry and didn't have your pizza. After all, you couldn't see the sauce being added or the delivery guy speeding down the highway. But just because you couldn't see it wouldn't have meant the miracle wasn't in the works.

Tell me that doesn't perfectly describe so many of our situations. When we are going through seasons of anxiety or depression and are crying out to God for help, it's easy to give up hope and determine that God either isn't there or isn't listening to our cries for help.

But God is always on the move, working *all things* together for good. It's just that we can't always see what he's up to. We order the pizza, but when it doesn't immediately arrive at our doorstep, we give up.

Don't lose hope.

God is listening to your prayers, but like preparing a pizza, sometimes there is a process to answering those prayers.

Think back to Joshua.

He put in the call for God to work a miracle—but he didn't see any results for quite some time. Why? It wasn't because God refused to answer his prayers or work in his life; it was just that there was more going on behind the scenes that Joshua couldn't see.

Or what about my story?

I called out for a miracle that day on the side of the highway, and guess what—nothing happened. At least from my vantage point. My friends still had to pick me up and take my guns. I still had to take a leave of absence and go to weeks of counseling. In that moment, I didn't feel like anything was happening.

But I can look back on that situation in the rearview mirror of my life and see that I was dead wrong. God was doing more miracles than I ever could've imagined.

God was putting together a process.

God was putting the right people in my life.

God was preparing me to experience more peace, more joy, and more freedom than I ever thought possible. God was working in my life; I just couldn't see it. And I'm telling you, that's what's happening in your situation right now.

Don't you ever forget that God is on the move.

You may not be able to see it, but he's at work in your life right now doing more than you could ever think or imagine. You have to remember: Truth #1: God is with you—even if you can't feel it.

*Truth #2: God is working—even if you can't see it.*

# GOD HAS A PLAN

I was thinking today how fun and helpful it would be if we could talk to Joshua and ask him to tell us about that day they crossed the Jordan and went into the promised land. I bet he'd tell us he was scared to death the whole time. He was already mourning the loss of Moses, and then suddenly, the weight of an entire nation was thrust on his shoulders. As the new leader, he was responsible for all those men, women, and children, and he was telling them to cross a river that couldn't be crossed unless God intervened. Meanwhile, for however long it took the water to dry up from Adam to where the priests were standing, Joshua had to endure stares from an entire nation of people who were probably starting to question whether he was the right guy for the job.

I'm getting anxious just thinking about that moment.

But he persevered. And because he did, he learned the same lesson you and I need to grab hold of right now. By the end of the day, when he saw the entire nation of Israel on the other side of the Jordan River, he realized that God had a plan all along.

That's our third and final truth we need to remember.

In the middle of the fight, when it feels like we are losing just as much ground as we are gaining, it can feel almost impossible to believe this final truth. But it's God's truth, so no matter how we feel at any given moment, we have to learn how to stand on it.

### Truth #3: God has a plan—even if you can't understand it.

In his Word, God reminded us, "'For I know the plans I have for you,' declares the LORD, 'plans to prosper you and not to harm you, plans to give you hope and a future'" (Jeremiah 29:11).

But let's be honest—in the middle of the storm, it's so easy to lose sight of that truth. Remember the very first verse we started this journey with back in chapter 1. "It is for freedom that Christ has set us free. *Stand firm*, then, and do not let yourselves be burdened again by a yoke of slavery" (Galatians 5:1, emphasis added).

Hopefully by now you see why Paul put such an emphasis on us learning to stand firm on these truths. Just because something is true doesn't mean we are always going to believe it. When anxiety and depression attack, they try to convince us to ignore God's truths.

This third truth isn't impacted by our circumstances. It doesn't change when we have a bad day. So sometimes we need to put aside our temporary feelings and stand on God's permanent truths!

I need you to see this right now. I need to encourage you or your loved one right now. *Just because you can't see what God is up to doesn't mean he doesn't have a plan.* Remember, you may not be able to see it, but his plan is in motion.

# GOD'S PLAN

This isn't just fancy church talk.

I've lived it.

And so can you.

The truth is, that day on the side of the road was not the first time I ever wanted to end my life. When I was twenty-four years old, one of my best friends tried to kill himself, and he taught me exactly how to do it. Around that time, I went through my first bout of depression, anxiety, and hopelessness.

It hit me hard.

I was a twenty-four-year-old drug and alcohol abuser who was heartbroken over a girl and was lost and drifting through life. Then one day, seemingly out of nowhere, I started having panic attacks. Occasionally, I'd have to pull my car over and get out just to breathe. I'd pace around my apartment, crying and just trying to survive the attacks. This went on for several days.

I wasn't sleeping.

I wasn't eating.

I was down fifteen pounds and didn't look good.

So I flew home to Kansas, where my mom lived, and I told her I was sorry for showing up. I just kept apologizing for how pathetic and desperate I was.

About three weeks after being in Kansas, I couldn't take the depression anymore. I didn't want anything to do with God at that point in my life, but when you are desperate, you are willing to try anything. My mom was a Christian, and since I was at her house and I had exhausted all my other ideas, I figured I might as well try prayer.

One day I went out to the backyard of her house, closed my eyes, and prayed: *God, if you're real, I need you to change something right this second. Please do something in my life. I can't live this way. If you're real, I need help. Now!*

I didn't feel anything.

I didn't see anything.

I didn't hear anything.

No goosebumps. No fireworks in the sky. No voices from heaven.

Which I took to be a sign that God either wasn't there or had better things to do with his time than listen to me complain.

I was on my own.

So I decided to take measures into my own hands. I had a bottle of pills up in my room that I knew would do the trick, so I ran up, grabbed them, and then dumped them out across the kitchen table. Then I poured myself a giant glass of water, sat down at the table, and just stared at them for a while.

And then I began to take some.

Between sips of water, I remember sobbing and shaking uncontrollably. It was beginning to sink in that this was the end. Suddenly a thought hit me out of nowhere. My mom had taken me to church a few times as a kid, and I had heard about heaven and hell. I knew enough to know that heaven was the good place, and hell was the bad place.

And that was about the extent of my knowledge.

But as I thought about it, I realized if heaven and hell were real, I was about thirty minutes away from being in one of them, and at the time, I wasn't sure what it took to get to the good place. So, I put down the pills and the glass, and I called an old college roommate.

I hadn't talked to him in a while, but I'd heard he had gotten involved in a church. That day he convinced me not to do anything stupid. Then he flew me to Illinois, where he lived, and brought me to a church service where I experienced the presence of God for the first time in my life. That day I asked God to forgive me of my sins and become part of my life.

That was the day everything began to change, but that wasn't even the craziest part.

Fast-forward a couple of years later. I was sitting in a church auditorium having a conversation with a girl named Jill, with whom I was in love.

Jill and I couldn't have been more opposite. She grew up in the church. She'd never walked away from her faith. She'd never made major bad decisions. She was a virgin when we got married.

Like I said, we were pretty much opposites.

We were engaged at the time, but today, we've been married for over twenty years. Over the last two decades, we've had so many memorable moments and conversations. But this one stands out above the rest.

Are you ready for this?

I'm telling you this is really something.

We were planning the wedding because that's all you do when you're engaged. It's all you talk about every waking second. Jill was flipping through the calendar when all of a sudden, she blurted out, "I knew you were going to ask me to marry you."

"Huh?"

"When we first met," she continued confidently. "I knew you were going to ask me to marry you."

"No, you didn't!"

"Yes, I did."

"How?"

Then she handed me the calendar and said, "What was the date when you tried to kill yourself?"

"I don't remember the exact day," I told her (things were a little hazy back then). "But this is the week I sat down at a table to kill myself."

"I knew it," she said with a smile as she looked up.

"I'm sorry?"

Holding back emotions, she explained how that very week, God woke her up in the middle of the night and put a thought in her mind that was so strong she couldn't ignore it.

"God told me I needed to start praying for my future husband. That I needed to start praying for him right now and that he wasn't the boy I was currently dating."

She went on to explain that the feeling was so strong she went and told her mom, "Mom, I can't explain this, but I just know God needs us to be praying for my future husband right now, and it's not the boy I'm dating."

How wild is that?

I was sitting at a table in Kansas about to kill myself, positive God either wasn't there or didn't care. But not only did God care, he loved me so much that he had two prayer warriors battling for my life on the other side of the country. He had two women I wouldn't meet for several months praying for my life, interceding in the name of God, and I didn't even know it.

God loved me—I just didn't know it.

Got had a plan—I just couldn't see it.

God was working in my life—I just couldn't feel it.

God had a fantastic future in store for me—I just didn't understand it.

If I'd given up that day, if I'd gone through with my suicidal intentions, I would've missed the greatest part of my life.

I never would've met Jill, the love of my life.

I never would've had the honor of raising the three sons I love so much it hurts.

I never would've become a pastor.

I never would've been part of our incredible church.

I never would've had the great satisfaction and joy of writing this book and helping people just like you and your loved ones as you go through the very same thing that almost took me out.

If I would've given up that day, I would've missed out on the greatest part of my life. I thought my life was over, but I was just getting started!

And I believe that's what God wants you to remember right now. This is not the end. Your story and your life are not over. He has plans and a hope and a future in store for you that will absolutely blow you away.

If you are feeling down-and-out right now—I get it.

If you've suffered a few blows and don't feel like fighting anymore—I get it.

If you are ready to throw in the towel—trust me, I get it.

But just because you lose a few battles doesn't mean you are going to lose this war. God isn't done with you yet, not even close. Remember, the battle is not going to be easy. This book is about the fight because that's literally what this is—a battle for your freedom.

Anxiety and depression are going to attack, but now you are armed with some life-changing, freedom-finding, and God-given weapons to attack back. It's time to step into the arena and go to battle. Even if you've taken a few hits and want to give up, it's time to remember who you are and who is fighting with you.

Get back in the fight and continue battling against your anxiety and depression—because this time around, you are armed with some serious artillery you didn't have before. Don't you dare throw in the towel. Don't you dare give up. And don't you ever forget these three truths:

1. God is with you—even if you can't feel it.
2. God is working—even if you can't see it.
3. God has a plan—even if you can't understand it.

# CONCLUSION

## *Your Time to Live Is Now!*

"But I'm not fixed yet. What do I do?"

That was the burning question I had for my counselor. After two weeks of prayer and worship in Alabama and then seven weeks of intensive counseling and therapy out of state, I'd finally made it home to Denver. It felt amazing to get home and be with my family again, and I took a few more months off work to slowly reintegrate back into the real world.

One of the best decisions I made after returning home was to find an amazing counselor to meet with once a week.

"I'm not fixed yet," I said again to him. "But I've been off work for five months. I either need to go back to leading one of the largest churches in the country or quit my job. I'm just scared to go back because I'm still messed up. I don't know what to do." What I was really trying to say was, "I can't start living a life God has called me to yet because I'm still too messed up!"

As I sat in my counselor's office in Colorado, I was so much healthier and stronger than I'd ever thought I would be. I didn't even recognize the version of myself that broke down by the side of the road; I had come so far. There were days where I felt great and times when I experienced peace, joy, confidence, and freedom on levels I'd never thought possible.

However, I was still far from perfect. I still did (and still do) have bad days and moments where I felt anxiety and depression tugging on my shirttail. And every time those feelings crept back up, my only thought was, *I'm not fixed yet.*

"Shawn, whose church is this?" my counselor asked.

"It's God's church," I told him.

"Okay, so pretend you were God for a second. Who would you want running this particular part of his church called Red Rocks Church?"

I had to think about that.

"If you were God," he continued, "would you want a guy running this church who thought he was perfectly put together, had all the answers, and didn't need to lean on your strength at all? Or would you want the guy who knew he was broken and whose only option was to lean on you to walk in his calling?"

"I guess I would want the broken guy leading," I said. "That way, he'd have to trust me."

"Exactly," my counselor said with a smile.

Let this free you up. Let my counselor counsel you right now.

He looked at me and said, "Shawn, God only uses broken people. God only uses broken leaders. Because what other kinds are there?"

He was reminding me what I've tried to remind you throughout this book—it's okay to not be okay. We're all broken; we're just broken differently. Nobody gets to be perfect at anything until heaven.

When it comes to my anxiety and depression, I will continue

to get healthier, better, and stronger every day, and I will continue to experience more and more peace, joy, confidence, and freedom in my life.

But I won't be perfect.

And neither will you.

If we sit around and wait until we're perfect before we begin walking in our God-given callings, we will never get off our couches. We don't have to have it all together before we begin pursuing our God-given dreams. Our time to start living is now!

We are all broken.

And we can walk in our God-given callings today.

Both statements are true because our brokenness is the place where God meets us. That's where his power shows up and his grace is sufficient. That's where our lives and our dreams take place. My counselor was reminding me that day what I want to remind you of today—your time to live is now!

## HEALTHY VERSUS HEALTHIER

The principles in this book will help you get *healthier*.

But notice the language I just used. I didn't say they will help you get *healthy*; I said they will help you get *healthier*. That may feel like a small change, but that small change made a world of difference for me.

While I was away, people in my life would say things like, "I can't wait until you're done with counseling and you're *healthy*." And these statements would cause me to panic. Healthy is an end-game. It's a finish line. And it was an unrealistic pressure for me. If I'd had to be perfect before I left inpatient counseling, I wouldn't have ever left. And if I'd had to be fixed before I returned to work, I would be unemployed.

When you are talking to people who struggle with anxiety and depression, don't use the word *healthy*—use *healthier*.

I'll never forget how relieved I felt the day a counselor helped me with this language. I may not be all the way there yet, but I am certainly getting *healthier*. It may be helpful to explain this to your family members and your loved ones. Remember, they want to help. They just may not be sitting around reading books about mental health. Explain it to them. Once you help people see the difference, they'll be able to adjust their language and expectations.

Counseling will help you get *healthier*.

The exercises in this book will help you get *healthier*.

Putting in the hard work will help you get *healthier*.

It's so important that we get this. You may not be where you want to be yet, but you also aren't where you used to be. You may be broken, but that doesn't mean you aren't getting better. If you are applying the principles in this book, you are getting *healthier* every day!

# PAIN AND PURPOSE

You don't have to wait until perfection before you start walking in your calling. The fact that you aren't perfect yet can make you even more effective as you step into the plans God has for your life. And again, I'm not talking about *someday*; I'm talking about *today*.

Remember Revelation 12:11?

Back in chapter 2, we found out there are two things that defeat the Enemy. The first is the blood Jesus shed for us when he died on the cross to forgive our sins, and the second is the power of our testimonies.

Your story is powerful.

Whenever I go through a difficult season, I always remind myself that my pain will become my platform. Because anytime I go through a struggle, I also know I'm going to turn around and share the experience with those who struggle. That's the reason I wrote this book. God changes people's lives, and oftentimes, he uses our stories to do it.

When we share our testimonies, we take the very thing Satan thought he would use to take *us* out and instead use it to take *him* out. One of the first steps to walking in our newfound callings is deciding to turn our pain into a platform.

But don't just share the pain; share the progress too. That's the formula for a great story that God will use to change lives. The more generous you are with your story, your pain, and the lessons you've learned along the way, the more God will use your testimony to set other people free.

I'm telling you—it will happen.

Let's read one more passage from Paul. As we've discussed at length, Paul not only experienced a ton of progress but also endured an awful lot of pain along the way. His testimony was full of tests. He wrote, "Praise be to the God and Father of our Lord Jesus Christ, the Father of compassion and the God of all comfort, who comforts us in all our troubles, so that we can comfort those in any trouble with the comfort we ourselves receive from God" (2 Corinthians 1:3–4).

God comforts us in our troubles so that we can pass that comfort along to others. God has not only helped me through all my trials but also brought me a ton of comfort along the way. I'm going to turn around and share that story with everyone I can because that's how we attack back!

*Today is the day to turn your pain into purpose!*

# I'VE GOT THIS

In the last chapter, I told you about my first set of severe panic attacks and the suicidal thoughts that came with it. I was twenty-four years old at the time and was living in Los Angeles, California. In the middle of that crisis, a friend brought me to a church service that transformed my life. I literally still had cocaine in my pocket when I walked in, but I walked out completely changed.

I can't tell you how incredible it was to experience the presence of God that first time. It caught me so off guard that I remember telling myself—*I'm going to spend the rest of my life helping other people experience this.*

I had no idea what that meant. I just knew it was what I wanted to do.

Fast-forward a few months, and I decided to move to Illinois just to be around the church and some people who were pursuing God. None of my friends in LA were heading that direction, and I knew enough to know that if I wanted to change the direction of my life, I needed to change the people in my life.

Late one night, about six weeks into my time in Illinois, I got a phone call from one of the church's youth pastors. Remember, I was a young kid who had been following God for a couple of months. And a few months earlier, I'd been having such bad panic attacks that I became suicidal.

I wouldn't say I was healthy. Far from it. But I was stronger and healthier than I had been ninety days earlier. I was on the journey toward freedom.

"We need you," the youth pastor said. And then he gave me an address to an apartment and asked if I could rush over.

My first thought was: *Oh, dear Lord, this pastor is someone with a secret drug addiction and needs my help finding some. This is not good.*

My second thought was: *What could they possibly need my help with? I've barely started figuring any of this God stuff out. I'm not ready.*

But I sped over to the apartment and quickly found out it belonged to a young man from the church who was dealing with such severe anxiety and depression that he was ready to take his own life.

The pastors told me his story, then explained that they just didn't know what to do or say. They'd never been through that type of anxiety; they'd never experienced depression; they'd never had suicidal thoughts. They wanted to help this young man but had no idea how. They were panicked, but the more they explained the situation, the more confident I got.

"I've got this," I said, cutting them off. I rolled up my sleeves and told all those pastors to get out of the room and let me go to work.

"Look," I said, sitting down across from the young man. "I don't just kind of know how you feel. I know exactly how you feel."

Then I started telling him my story.

"I also know that your feelings are lying to you right now, your emotions are lying to you, and that you really don't want to end your life. You really just want to be better and healthier and stronger. And I am a walking, talking example of that being a possibility for you." I didn't articulate it exactly the same way back then, but what I basically shared with him was: "You are not crazy. You are not alone. And this will end."

His face began to soften.

"You're going to look back on this moment and be so glad you didn't do anything stupid," I told him. And I meant it. "I'm telling you: you're going to get through this."

Then I told him I was pretty new to this whole God thing, but I'd walked into a church a few months ago and experienced the power of God in a way that changed me.

"I started feeling a peace that I never thought was possible," I told him. "I started feeling hope for the first time in a long time, and I started feeling confidence for the first time ever. And I bet if God would do that for me, he'd do it for you."

Then I asked him if he wanted to pray. And when he said yes, I called the pastors back into the room to do their thing.

Listen to me.

My past and my pain didn't disqualify me. They were the very things that gave me the authority I needed to speak into that young man's life. Because of my pain, I was able to help him in a way that a bunch of professional pastors couldn't.

My specific *pain* turned into my specific *platform*.

I was able to help someone who was about to *take* his life, *give* his life to following God. Talk about purpose. Talk about self-worth. I hadn't felt those feelings in years, but when I started embracing my story (my unfinished, unfixed story), I discovered why I'm here on this planet.

I'm telling you right now—that is where you are headed. God does not waste anything. If you allow him, he will take your greatest pain and turn it into a platform—into an opportunity for you to help people.

One person at a time.

You are about to experience a newfound purpose. You don't have to wait till you're "fixed" to start helping people. You can do it now.

While you're broken.

While you're a mess.

While you're on a journey.

Because after all, those three statements describe every one of us. We aren't there yet. We are all works in progress. But we are getting better, stronger, and healthier every day!

The day you choose to look around the world and find some people who are struggling with the same thing you've struggled with, everything will begin to change. Look for ways to encourage them, inspire them, and walk with them. I guarantee your time and energy will be worth it. Even though you are still a work in progress, you can help people in ways you never thought possible. Which will bring you purpose, which will lead to peace, joy, hope, and confidence. And those things automatically begin to push away anxiety and depression. And the beauty of this is, it can all start today. Remember: your time to live is now!

## YES, YOU CAN!

You can do this. Seriously. I know the battle is scary, but now you have the resources and weapons you need to begin winning. Anxiety and depression are extremely real—and they almost always go together. If you (or a loved one) experience one, odds are you experience them both. But freedom is possible. Anxiety may attack, but you can attack back. You can do this; you just have to put these principles to work.

It all begins with three things you need to know:

1. You are not crazy.
2. You are not alone.
3. This will end.

This is not going to be the end of your story. It might be an ongoing battle, but you will continually get better, healthier, and stronger. It might be a lifelong journey, but peace and joy and hope and confidence are on the way.

My guess is you've already begun to experience this freedom to some degree as you've gone through this book. You can't come face-to-face with the Word of God and the truth about mental illness and not begin to see a transformation in your life.

The next step is to realize God has given us some powerful weapons. We just need to start using them in the battle of overcoming anxiety and depression.

Worship is a weapon, and prayer is powerful. Start using them to fight back. Tell God exactly how you feel. Don't sugarcoat it. Be real, raw, and honest with him. Ask him for the freedom you desire and the peace you are craving. But then don't forget to thank him. That constant choice to be thankful, that continual decision to worship, is what begins to usher in the peace, hope, joy, and confidence. And that's what you and all your loved ones need right now more than anything, so put these weapons to use!

And don't forget that anxiety is not a solo battle. Remember what God has brought you through; remember what he's promised you; and remember that he's going with you. Assemble an army. Get the right people around you, and be fully honest and transparent with them. Let them know the depths of your depression and anxiety, and tell them practical ways they can fight with you. Your freedom depends on this, so choose a wise, God-fearing army and get them into the battle.

Don't just read about these weapons—start using them.

In addition to these good things we need to *start* doing, there are some harmful things we need to *stop* doing.

Stop hiding the depths of your pain and pretending you're okay. If your situation calls for it, get professional help and begin to heal from your past. If you're harboring unforgiveness over some past grievances, do the difficult work of forgiveness. It almost sounds counterintuitive, especially when dealing with depression and anxiety, but the fruit of forgiveness is peace. And we all need some peace right now.

Stop performing for your critics. You can't make everyone happy, and the more influence God gives you in this world, the more people will criticize what you do. It's not pleasant, but it's also not the end of the world. Decide right now that you aren't going to allow critical voices and the comparison game to usher in new levels of anxiety and depression. Instead, start reminding yourself what your Creator says about you, what you're capable of, and what kind of victory you are headed toward.

And finally, remember this is a lifelong journey. You aren't going to get it perfect all the time. But the goal isn't to arrive; it's to continue the journey. It isn't about being strong; it's about getting *stronger*. It isn't about getting healthy; it's about getting *healthier*. Along the way, when things get tough, remember:

- God is with you—even if you can't feel it.
- God is working—even if you can't see it.
- God has a plan—even if you can't understand it.

You have an incredible opportunity in front of you to begin changing the world one person at a time. Yes, you are still broken, but you are getting better.

So yes, you can overcome.

Yes, you can conquer.

Yes, you can change.

Yes, you can experience freedom.

Yes, you can experience healing.

Yes, you can turn your pain into purpose.

Yes, you can start to truly live *today*.

Don't let your pain become a prison—decide today that your pain will be your platform. And then watch as God opens up amazing experiences and incredible opportunities for you to help others by sharing your story and your life with the world. It's time to go live! As somebody who understands what it's like to deal with anxiety, depression, and hopelessness at an extremely deep level, let me remind you of this absolute truth:

Yes, you can!

# ACKNOWLEDGMENTS

I cannot say thank you enough to:

My wife, Jill. You stood by my side through all of this, and you never once judged me or made me feel wrong for suffering. There was never a moment where I doubted that you would be right there with me. Your strength, grace, and love are at levels I've never experienced before. I love you with all my heart.

My three boys, Ethan, Austin, and Ashton. I wasn't the only one who went through a painful season; the three of you did too. Along the way you never stopped encouraging me, and you never stopped believing in me, and I am forever grateful. God has bigger plans for your lives than you could ever even imagine, and I can't wait to watch them unfold!

My sister, Lorrie. When I was at my worst, you dropped everything and moved across the country to be with us. You made it possible for Jill and me to stay in the fight, knowing that our boys were in good hands. We may not have gotten through those dark months without all of your help. I love you!

Ryan Wekenman. Thank you for not only being my friend but also an incredible writer. You took my passionate thoughts, notes, and scribbles and turned it into something that looks like

I understand the English language. You made this thing possible. It is what it is in part because of you. I love you, bro.

Red Rocks Church. The support you showed me through all of this has been incredible. You walked beside me and refused to give up on me. I cannot tell you how grateful I am for the countless calls, texts, posts, and prayers. I love you, church!

Pastor Chris Hodges and the Highlands Church Family. You rolled out the red carpet for me during the most difficult days of my adult life. You didn't have time to do it, and you weren't going to get anything in return; you just did it. Thank you for opening up your home, office, life, church, and family. Your wisdom, guidance, and love gave me the courage to fight. I love you, PC. Layne, Dino, Mayo, Micahn, Dr. Record and the rest of the Highlands family . . . thank you and love you all!

Jimmy and Irene Rollins. You two have redefined what friendship means to me. It's not just that you showed up at the most pivotal times, when you didn't have to; it's that you've never stopped showing up for Jill and me ever since. Thank you for loving us, supporting us, and being such amazing friends. I love you, fam!

The Staff and Leadership Team at Red Rocks Church. You walked with me every step of the way and took on the weight of a very large and pressure-packed organization while I was gone. Thank you for having my back so that I could go through counseling, spend time with God, be with my family, and begin a healing process that would change my life forever. Worship team, thank you for writing songs for me. BZ, your daily scriptures and messages of encouragement fueled me in ways you will never know. And the constant phone calls, texts, and notes from all of you were game-changing. I love you all and am so grateful to get to be a part of this church family!

The Center. You know who you are. Your entire team cared for me, listened to me, loved me, and advised me through days when I didn't think I could go on living. I am eternally grateful.

Pastor Craig and Amy Groeschel. You're like a big brother and sister to Jill and me. You remind us that it's OK to not be OK sometimes. You've never left our side, no matter how bad things have gotten. And you've encouraged me along the way that I could actually write a book that helps other people even though I'm far from perfect. We love you so much!

Harv. You are a godsend in my life. Thank you for always being there for me!

The entire team at Thomas Nelson. You took a risk on someone like me. I know I am a handful to work with at times, but thank you for your hard work, guidance, and most of all, your patience. I'm so grateful for you all, and I can't wait for the world to see this book!

# APPENDIX

## *Panic Attack Survival Guide*

Earlier this week, a friend stumbled into my office and asked if we could talk. He was shaking, and I could tell he was trying hard to hold back all the emotions that wanted to come out. Before he said a word, I knew what was happening. I could tell because I've been there so many times before.

He was having a panic attack.

My knee-jerk reaction was to talk to him about everything in this book. I wanted to help him put together a long-term battle plan for his freedom. But I realized in that moment that wasn't what he needed. He was in a tailspin and needed some immediate attention.

If you or your loved one is currently having a panic attack, putting together a long-term plan for freedom is probably not your top priority. Once things calm down, you can talk about winning the war, but first, you need to win the battle that is right in front of you.

This appendix is a panic attack survival guide. I'm going to give you five things to do if you are having a panic attack and five things to do if you are trying to help a loved one through a panic attack. This is some of the most practical advice I ever learned about anxiety and depression. It's gotten me through extremely pivotal and scary moments. When your emotions take over, and the lies start whispering that this will never end, practicality is exactly what you need.

You need a battle plan.

You need a panic attack survival guide.

When Jill called one of my pastors in Alabama the day I broke down on the side of the road, *triage* was the word he used. He told me to get to Alabama because we needed to assess the damage. Their church has a team trained to be first responders. They go into cities when hurricanes hit to bring relief. He explained that when they first go in, and the dust is still settling, triage is step one. Long before you start helping people rebuild their lives, you first have to get them to safety.

That's why I've included this appendix in this book. I want to help get you to safety right now. The rest of the book will help you rebuild your life, but first, you need to deal with the panic attack that is right in front of you.

When my friend came into my office, he needed immediate help. If you or a loved one is in the same boat, here are some immediate steps you can take. Let's talk about how to help yourself first, and then we'll talk about helping someone else.

# HOW TO HELP YOURSELF

The first thing you have to understand about panic attacks is that they happen in your mind and body. I find it helpful to separate the two. I usually feel the panic creep into my body first. My chest tightens, I feel a shortness of breath, and I start to feel like I'm suffocating. Then the body signals the mind, telling me it's time to have a full-blown panic attack.

The mind and the body are connected.

Other times, my panic attacks seem to work the other way. The panic starts in my mind, which triggers my body's fight-or-flight mentality. Then my body starts tightening up, and I have to remember I'm not suffocating—my chest muscles are just tightening up. My body temperature increases, my blood pressure goes up, and I start to sweat. It's all the stuff my body was created to do in actual life-threatening situations.

Either way, the mind and body work together to create a horrifying experience. The body goes into fight or flight, the mind spins faster and faster, and before you know it, you're in the middle of an inner hurricane that no one else can see. Which is why we feel like no one else will ever understand.

I know the feeling. Trust me. I know it all too well. Over the years, I've also learned several amazing techniques to survive once it hits. Next time it hits, here's what I want you to do.

### Step #1: Slow Your Breathing on Purpose

The first thing to focus on is your breathing. Slow, long exhales send signals from your body to your mind, telling it to begin to relax. I'm not an expert, and I won't pretend to know all the vocabulary or understand *why* this works (just google it if you want to know). But even if I don't know exactly *why* this works, I can tell you firsthand that it *does*.

Try breathing in for a count of four, then exhale for a count of five.

The exact count isn't the point; the goal is intentionally slow-ing your breathing. For me, I make my exhale slightly longer than my inhale because that long, slow exhale is when my body seems to send signals to my mind that everything is okay, so it can relax and unwind.

### Step #2: Change Your Scenery

The next step is to change your scenery. You may not know why you are having a panic attack, but your present surroundings obviously aren't helping. So go somewhere new. If I'm in my car, I'll pull over and get out. If I'm in my house, I'll walk outside. If I'm in an office building, I'll leave and go somewhere new.

Sometimes I'll head to the gym or walk down the hall and hop on an exercise bike. Or I'll walk out into my backyard for a second, look at some trees, and slow my breathing. In those moments, I'm wound up so tightly that I'm starting to go into a tailspin. Slowing my breathing and changing my scenery helps me unwind.

### Step #3: Take Your Mind Someplace Else

A big portion of a panic attack happens in your mind, and if you are anything like me, you can't stop thinking about the fact that the panic attack is happening while it's happening. But when we focus on it, we feed it. The more we dwell on it, the stronger it gets. The good news is, if we can take our minds someplace else, we'll stop feeding the panic. And if you stop feeding it, it loses its power.

The best thing we can do is—on purpose—take our minds someplace else. Anywhere else. Start counting blades of grass or ceiling tiles. Begin to notice what you can hear, then think about where the sounds are coming from. Notice what you can smell and think about that. Or start playing a game on your phone or reading something else that has nothing to do with your life.

My go-to is focusing on gratitude.

I usually put on worship music and start telling God about all the things I'm thankful for. I thank him for my amazing wife and kids. My friends. My job. My house. Or simply the fact that I have food and water today. I start saying thank you out loud because it takes my mind off the panic and focuses it back on peace. And in the middle of a panic attack, that's exactly what I need.

You don't have to copy my strategy, but you do need to have one. Decide ahead of time how you are going to take your mind someplace else when the panic comes. And when it does, slow your breathing, change your scenery, and then take your mind someplace else.

### Step #4: Stop Fighting

This next step may sound counterintuitive, but I want you to *stop* fighting against the panic attack. One day in counseling, I was having an attack. I was pacing around the room really fast, grunting, yelling, and crying. My fists were clenched, and I was doing everything I could to try to fight off the attack.

One of the counselors said something I'll never forget. He told me trying to fight off a panic attack is like being stuck in a giant hole with a shovel and deciding you are going to dig your way out. When you attempt to actively fight off a panic attack, all you do is dig yourself a deeper hole.

My friend Marc coaches a professional mixed martial arts team. For obvious reasons, his fighters often feel a lot of anxiety before fights and even have panic attacks. When that happens, he doesn't tell them to fight the panic. Instead, he tells them to *make friends with it.*

Talk to the feeling. Notice where in the body the panic attack is coming from. That may sound strange, but it works. For me, I've realized depression seems to land in the pit of my stomach, but anxiety hits me in the chest. Noticing this helps me remind myself that I'm not suffocating or dying—my chest muscles are just tightening up. Suddenly, I don't feel a need to fight the feeling; I can welcome it. I begin having a conversation with my anxiety that goes something like this: *I understand you're here right now. I'm not happy about it, but I also know you're going to leave soon.*

I know that sounds weird, but try it. It's a way to remind yourself you are not your anxiety. You are not your depression. Those are just feelings and emotions. They're not who you are. Make friends with the panic while it's there. Stop fighting. Acknowledge it, notice where it is taking place in your body, and then watch it leave.

## Step #5: Use Your Imagination

The final step is to start using your imagination. Your imagination is powerful—use it to your advantage. Picture your panic as clouds in the sky slowly moving toward the horizon. Or as a train slowly passing you by.

When I was a kid in Kansas, I remember sitting out on random country roads for what felt like hours, waiting for a train to pass. Slowly but surely the boxcars would go by, and eventually, they would move right out of sight. The gates would come up, and I'd be free to move on about my day again.

That's exactly how I picture my panic attacks.

Once I've slowed my breathing, changed my scenery, taken

my mind and focus someplace else, and made friends with the anxiety, I begin to picture it like the caboose of the train passing by. It may have blocked my road for a minute, but now it is slowly heading off toward the horizon. Then the gates in front of me begin to rise, and I get to go on with my day.

Begin to picture your anxiety like one of those slow trains moving off in the distance, and accept the fact that peace is coming back. Relaxation is coming back. Calm is coming back. Think, *The anxiety that I'm not fighting against has decided to slowly leave, and now I'm going to continue with my day.*

# HOW TO HELP A LOVED ONE

Now the question is: How do you help a loved one through a panic attack? This is huge. Since I've gone public with my friends, family, and church about my panic attacks, I can't tell you how many times people have asked for advice on helping a loved one get through the same things I've been going through. I love that question. That's a skill we should all have. Because odds are, at some point in your life, someone you love will go through a panic attack. I want to coach you through this because you can play a pivotal role in helping them get through one of the most challenging moments of their entire life. If a loved one is going through a panic attack, here are five things you can do to help.

### Step #1: Be Present

The number one and most important thing you can do for a loved one in the middle of a panic attack is to simply be there. That may sound intimidating to you at first. You may be thinking:

*I don't know what to do.*

*I don't know what to say.*

*What if I make things worse?*

But I can promise you from firsthand experience, you simply being there with them is of the utmost importance. The only thing worse than having a panic attack is having a panic attack by yourself. That's when those terrible thoughts of ending your life begin to set in. If someone you love has a panic attack, don't leave them alone.

When we moved to Denver seventeen years ago to start a church, there was nobody in the church because it didn't exist. Which also meant there were no paychecks for the pastors of the "church." So we all got side jobs to pay our bills. I became the graveyard-shift chaplain at a local hospital. If anyone's vital signs flatlined, I got called (often in the middle of the night) and had to drive to the hospital. Most of the time, it was about three o'clock in the morning, and I would get in my car and drive to work, knowing that someone had just passed away and my job was to be with the family.

I'll never forget my first day of on-the-job training. We were about to walk into a room occupied by a young couple who had just lost their child during childbirth. I was a father of two very young children at the time and was absolutely shaken to the core and heartbroken for this family. I couldn't pull it together or stop crying.

"I don't know what to do in there," I said to the woman training me before we walked in. "I don't know what to say or how to act."

"Your job is not to have the perfect words or actions," she responded calmly, with a reassuring smile. "This is called the ministry of presence. We're going to walk into this room and just be present with them because they are going through the worst night of their lives and need people to be present with them."

*The ministry of presence.*

I love that line. It's always stuck with me. Your presence is powerful. Being present is the number one thing you can do for your loved one. Even if you don't do a thing or say a word, your presence can be a huge help, so sacrifice whatever else you had going on and be with them.

## Step #2: Don't Pretend You Understand What You Don't Understand

Please don't throw out quick fixes or your idea of solutions, especially if you've never had a panic attack. Just be with your loved one.

Jill and I are good friends with a couple who have experienced this tension. The wife struggles with panic attacks, but the husband is one of the most peaceful people I've ever met. He's never had a panic attack, so he doesn't understand what they feel like. They were telling me that one night recently, she woke up in the middle of the night and was having an earthshaking panic attack. He woke up, realized what was going on, and said, "Oh babe, you'll be okay." As he rolled over to fall back to sleep, he added, "Just take a TUMS."

I love my friend, but please don't ever do that. What I know from the advice he gave his spouse is that he simply doesn't understand the severity of panic attacks.

That's okay.

But if you don't understand, don't pretend like you do. Don't give straight answers or quick-fix solutions that, in your mind, make sense. Because I promise you, that's not what they need. And if you try to pretend like you know how they feel, they will realize it from a mile away.

They will put walls up and shut you down.

You don't have to know what they're going through to love them, and you don't have to know what a panic attack feels like to support them. Don't pretend to understand what you don't understand; just be present.

### Step #3: Create a Safe and Judgment-Free Space

Shame is one of the hidden enemies that will try to destroy your loved one during their attack. It's embarrassing to let someone you love see you in the middle of a battle. In the middle of a panic attack, shame takes over your mind and tries to convince you that it's all your fault, that you are broken and are a burden to your loved ones.

Go out of your way to let the person you are supporting know that it is perfectly okay to struggle. Let them know the panic is normal and it's not going to last forever. Let them know that they are safe to be themselves and safe to express their feelings.

They are safe to cry.

They are safe to yell.

They are safe to walk around the room.

They are safe to be illogical in the moment because you love them so much.

Create a safe and judgment-free space for them to let it all out. And please don't make the mistake of thinking just because you said it once, they get it. Believe me, if they are in the middle of a panic attack, they'll need to hear it over and over again because shame will be trying to inch into their mind to convince them that they are a burden. You get to combat that by reinforcing that you love them, aren't embarrassed by them, and aren't going any-where. Because you are a safe and judgment-free space.

## Step #4: Remind

There's a reason I started this book with the three things you need to know. Those weren't just for you. They are for your loved one as well:

1. You are not crazy.
2. You are not alone.
3. This will end.

Remind your loved one of those three things as often as you can. In fact, if you can't think of any other words to say, just start repeating those three phrases over and over again.

As I mentioned earlier, when my friend came into my office I wanted to help him put together a long-term battle plan to fight for his freedom. But that's not what he needed. At least, not at that moment. So instead, I just looked at him and said, "You are not crazy. You are not alone. This will end."

Then I went on to tell him there were tons of people right in this building who had panic attacks and that he just didn't know it because so many people are embarrassed to talk about it. Remember, the CDC tells us that almost half of all Americans will struggle with something like this.

Almost half! You are not crazy.

Then I reminded him that he was not alone. I told him I was right there with him and wasn't going anywhere. And finally, I reminded him that this would not last forever. This was not the end of his story, not even close.

Those three statements were enough.

As I mentioned before, as soon as he took in those words, he broke. The tears began to flow, the conversation started, and you could almost see the pressure begin to release as he finally exhaled, shut out the lies, and started to take in the truth that he is completely normal. He's just broken like the rest of us. He deals with anxiety, and that's okay!

Helping your loved one understand those three things and reminding them often will bring an amazing amount of peace to an unpeaceful situation. Just keep saying them: "You are not crazy. You are not alone. This will end."

### Step #5: Keep Showing Up

On behalf of every single one of us who has ever felt the inner turmoil of a panic attack, thank you for even being willing to read about these steps. You did that because you want to help, and I can't tell you how powerful your presence can be. We don't need you to do anything profound; we just need your presence.

Show up, don't pretend you understand it if you've never experienced it, create a safe and judgment-free space for us, and keep reminding us of the three truths we need to know. Then do it all over and over again. It doesn't matter if it's your child, sibling, spouse, friend, coworker, or teammate—your presence is more valuable than you know.

*Keep showing up!*

Your willingness to be present in the middle of your loved one's struggle can be a catalyst to helping them find more health, wholeness, and freedom than they ever thought possible.

# NOTES

1. "Learn More," Red Rocks Church, accessed June 5, 2021, https://
   www.redrockschurch.com/learn-more/.
2. "Learn About Mental Health," Centers for Disease Control and
   Prevention, January 26, 2018, https://www.cdc.gov/mentalhealth
   /learn/index.htm.
3. Bessel van der Kolk, *The Body Keeps the Score: Brain, Mind, and Body
   in the Healing of Trauma* (New York: Penguin Books, 2014), 235.
4. "Data and Publications," Centers for Disease Control and
   Prevention, January 26, 2018, https://www.cdc.gov/mentalhealth
   /data_publications/.
5. Levi Lusko, "Nothing Healthy Grows in the Dark," Levi Lusko
   (website), August 23, 2011, https://levilusko.com/nothing-healthy
   -grows-in-the-dark/.
6. Theodore Roosevelt, *The Man in the Arena: Selected Writings of
   Theodore Roosevelt*, ed. Brian Thomsen (New York: Tom Doherty
   Associates, 2003), 5.

# ABOUT THE AUTHOR

SHAWN JOHNSON serves as lead pastor of Red Rocks Church in Denver, Colorado, a community he and a small group of people started in 2005 that has grown to include nine different campuses. Red Rocks Church has been on *Outreach* magazine's Fastest Growing Churches and Largest Participating Churches lists many times. Shawn has spoken at a variety of conferences, events, ministries, and other churches, including C3 Conference, Leadership Network, RightNow Media, Experience Conference, ARC Conferences, and many others. Shawn and his wife, Jill, have three active sons, Ethan, Austin, and Ashton, so when they're not at church, they're usually watching or playing sports.